German

Learn German For Beginners Including German Grammar, German Short Stories and 1000+ German Phrases

© Copyright 2018

All rights Reserved. No part of this book may be reproduced in any form without permission in writing from the author. Reviewers may quote brief passages in reviews.

Disclaimer: No part of this publication may be reproduced or transmitted in any form or by any means, mechanical or electronic, including photocopying or recording, or by any information storage and retrieval system, or transmitted by email without permission in writing from the publisher.

While all attempts have been made to verify the information provided in this publication, neither the author nor the publisher assumes any responsibility for errors, omissions or contrary interpretations of the subject matter herein.

This book is for entertainment purposes only. The views expressed are those of the author alone, and should not be taken as expert instruction or commands. The reader is responsible for his or her own actions.

Adherence to all applicable laws and regulations, including international, federal, state and local laws governing professional licensing, business practices, advertising and all other aspects of doing business in the US, Canada, UK or any other jurisdiction is the sole responsibility of the purchaser or reader.

Neither the author nor the publisher assumes any responsibility or liability whatsoever on the behalf of the purchaser or reader of these materials. Any perceived slight of any individual or organization is purely unintentional.

Contents

CHAPTER 1 – PRONUNCIATION 3
    Learning the German alphabet 3
CHAPTER 2 – THE BASICS 8
    Nouns - main words 8
    Forming the plural 8
CHAPTER 3 – PRONOUNS 16
OVERVIEW OF GERMAN PRONOUNS 16
    What are personal pronouns? 17
    Exercise 19
    What are possessive pronouns? 20
    What are relative pronouns? 23
    Exercise 24
    What are reflexive pronouns? 25
    Exercise 26
    What are demonstrative pronouns? 26
    Exercise 28
    What are indefinite pronouns? 28
    Exercise 31
    What are interrogative pronouns? 31
    Exercise 32
    Exercise 34
CHAPTER 4 – SENTENCE CONSTRUCTION 35
    Declarative sentence 35
    Interrogative sentence 35
CHAPTER 5 – GERMAN VERBS 40
    Present 41

- Exercise 42
- What is the preterite? 43
- Exercise 45
- The Perfect 45
- Exercise 46
- Future 1 and 2 47
- Exercise 48
- What is the plusquamperfect? 48
- Exercise 50
- What are modal verbs? 50
- Exercise 51
- What are reflexive verbs? 52
- Exercise 53
- What is active and passive? 53
- Exercise 55
- Participle 1 and 2 55
- Exercises 57
- Subjunctive 1 and 2 58
- Exercise 60
- What is an imperative? 60
- Exercise 62

CHAPTER 6 – WHAT ARE ADJECTIVES? 63
- Definite article 63
- Indefinite article 64
- No article 64
- Exercise 64
- What are adverbs? 65
  - *4 different types of adverbs:* 65
- Exercise 66

CHAPTER 7 – WHAT ARE PREPOSITIONS? 67
- Exercise 69

CHAPTER 8 – NUMBERS, DATE AND TIME 71

CHAPTER 9 - GERMAN ON THE ROAD 78

THE JOURNEY BY TRAIN	78
WITH THE CAR TO THE AIRPORT	79
TRAVEL BY PLANE	80
THE GAS STATION	81
HOTEL	82
THE FRONT DESK	83
RESTAURANT	85
RESTAURANT ARRIVAL	85
ORDERING DESSERT	87
INTRODUCING YOURSELF AND MAKING PLANS	87
TO GREET/ TO SAY GOODBYE	88
ASK FOR HELP	88
HOW ARE YOU?	89
WHAT IS YOUR PHONE NUMBER?	89
TO ARRANGE TO MEET SOMEONE	90
AT THE POST OFFICE AND AT THE BANK	93

CHAPTER 10 – MOST COMMON WORDS 96

CONCLUSION 115

PART 2: GERMAN SHORT STORIES 116

9 SIMPLE AND CAPTIVATING STORIES FOR EFFECTIVE GERMAN LEARNING FOR BEGINNERS 116

INTRODUCTION 117

CHAPTER 1 – HOW TO READ EFFECTIVELY 118

CHAPTER 2 – DER MANN UND DAS PFERD (THE MAN AND THE HORSE) 120

CHAPTER 3 – DER TOTE SAMEN (THE DEAD SEED) 127

CHAPTER 4 – EIN WAHRER FREUND (A TRUE FRIEND) 135

CHAPTER 5 – SCHALEN AUS HOLZ (WOODEN BOWLS) 141

CHAPTER 6 – EINE BRÜCKE DES FRIEDENS (A PEACEFUL BRIDGE) 147

CHAPTER 7 – DU BIST WAS DU DENKST (YOU ARE WHAT YOU THINK) 153

CHAPTER 8 – DER TAXIFAHRER (THE TAXI DRIVER) 159

CHAPTER 9 – JULIA RETTET DEN KINDERGARTEN (JULIA SAVES THE KINDERGARTEN) 167

CHAPTER 10 – EIN WAHRER HELD (A TRUE HERO) 176

CONCLUSION 184

PART 3: GERMAN PHRASE BOOK 185

THE ULTIMATE GERMAN PHRASE BOOK FOR TRAVELERS OF GERMANY, INCLUDING OVER 1000 PHRASES FOR ACCOMMODATIONS, EATING, TRAVELING, SHOPPING, AND MORE 185

INTRODUCTION 186

CHAPTER 1 – PRONUNCIATION 188

CHAPTER 2 – STANDARD PHRASES IN GERMAN 191
- Everyday words 191
- Understanding 192
- Signs 192
- Greeting 192
- Saying "Bye" 193
- To apologize to someone / Thank someone 193
- Compliments 194
- How are you? 194
- Asking for opinions and expressing yourself 194
- Religion 195
- Traveling by public transport 196
- Getting to know each other 196
- Make an appointment 197
- Cursing 197
- Being upset with something/someone 198
- Events and activities 198

CHAPTER 3 – NUMBERS AND COLORS 200
- Time 201
- Time of the day 202
- Duration 202
- Days 202
- Months 203
- Colors 203

CHAPTER 4 – TRANSPORT 205
- Passport control and customs 205
- Bus and Train 206
- Direction 208
- Taxi 209

    Boat 210

CHAPTER 5 – ACCOMMODATION 214
    Finding accommodation 214
    Reservation 214
    Camping 216
    Complaints 217

CHAPTER 6 – MONEY 220

CHAPTER 7 – RESTAURANTS AND FOOD 221
    Reservation and Ordering 221
    Ordering snacks 223

CHAPTER 8 – BARS 227
    Ordering drinks 227
    Asking for internet and WiFi 229
    The day after 229
    Smoking 229

CHAPTER 9 – SHOPPING 233
    Making a decision 234
    Finding products 235
    At a hair salon 236

CHAPTER 10 – DRIVING 239

CHAPTER 11 – AUTHORITIES 246

CHAPTER 12 – EMERGENCIES 247
    Health 248
    At the pharmacy 248
    Visiting a doctor 249

CHAPTER 13 - SERVICES AND REPAIRS 262
    Photography 263
    Post office 263
    Bank 265
    ATM 267

CHAPTER 14 – SPARE TIME 270
    Teathre 270
    The club 271

  Flirting – Small Talk 272

  Museum and Gallery 273

CHAPTER 15 – USEFUL WORDS AND TERMS..279

CHAPTER 16 – TIPS FOR LEARNING A NEW LANGUAGE 296

CHAPTER 17 – BONUS – WRITING AN E-MAIL 300

CONCLUSION 303

Part 1: German

An Essential Guide to German Language Learning

Introduction

Whatever plans you may have for your future, with knowledge of the German language, you can create infinite possibilities. Learning German means acquiring skills to improve your professional and personal quality of life.

A global career: With German-language skills, you can improve your career prospects with German companies in your own country and in other countries. Good German skills make you a productive employee for an employer with global business relationships.

Tourism and hotel accommodation: Tourists from German-speaking countries travel far and wide, spending more on holiday than tourists from other countries. They are gladly introduced by German-speaking staff and German-speaking tour guides.

Science and research: German is the second most important language for science. With its contribution to research and development, Germany is third in the world in grant research fellowships to foreign scientists.

Communication: The developments in the media and information and communication technology require multilingual communication. A number of important websites are in German. Germany is ranked 6th in the world out of 87 countries, (just behind India, the UK, the USA, China and Russia) in the annual production of new books. Your knowledge of the German language, therefore, allows you to access more information.

Cultural understanding: Learning German means gaining an insight into the life, the wishes, and the dreams of people in German-speaking countries, with their multicultural society.

Travel: With your knowledge of German, you can expand your travel experiences not only in the German-speaking countries, but also in other European countries, especially Eastern Europe.

Enjoyment of literature, music, art and philosophy: German is the language of Goethe, Kafka, Mozart, Bach and Beethoven. Speaking German allows you to deepen the enjoyment of reading and / or listening of their works in their original language.

Study and work opportunities in Germany: Germany awards a large number of scholarships to study there. There are special visas for young foreigners, and there are special provisions for work permits for certain professions.

Exchange programs: There are exchange programs between students from Germany and many countries around the world.

In business life: Communication in German with your German-speaking business partners leads to better business relations and thus to better opportunities for effective communication - and thus to success.

All these reasons and more are why learning German is a great idea. Start your journey with this amazing book!

Chapter 1 – Pronunciation

Learning the German alphabet

The basis of any language is its alphabet. It would be kind of embarrassing if you could speak a language, but you couldn't really spell your own name. In this chapter, you will have the opportunity to learn what you absolutely need to know about the German alphabet, and you will get answers to questions such as:

What is a "Umlaut?"

When to use "ß" and when "ss?"

How do you pronounce "sch" and "ch?"

The German alphabet has 26 letters, just like the English alphabet. In addition, there are the following "umlauts" (gray): Ü, Ö, Ä and the ß.

A, Ä, B, C, D, E, F, G, H, I, J, K, L, M, N, O, Ö, P, Q, R, S, ß, T, U, Ü, V, W, X, Y, Z

Alphabet with pronunciation A/a [a:]

Ä/ä [ɛ:]

B/b [be:]

C/c [tse:]

D/d [de:]

E/e [e:]

F/f [ɛf]

G/g [Ge]

H/h [HA]

I/i [i]

J/j [jɔt]

K/k [ka:]

L/l [ɛl]

M/m [ɛm]

N/n [ɛn]

O/o [o:]

Ö/ö [O]

P/p [pe:]

Q/q [ku:]

R/r [ɛr]

S/s [ɛs]

ß [ɛs'tsɛt]

T/t [te:]

U/u [u:]

Ü/ü [y:]

V/v [faʊ]

W/w [unit:]

X/x [ICS]

Y/y ['iupsilɔn]

Z/z [tsɛt]

Vowels

In the German alphabet there are 8 vowels.

A, E, I, O and U, and 3 Umlauts, Ä, Ü, Ö.

These are formed by two successive vowels:

Ü,ü   U+E   (Bücher)

Ä, ä   A+E (Länder)

Ö, ö   O+E (Brötchen)

Diphthongs

Diphthongs are two consecutive vowels. "Ei" and "ai" sound the same, like "eu" and "äu." To figure out when to use which diphthong, it is helpful to form the word stem. "Mäuse (Mice)," for example, is formed from "Maus (Mouse)"; therefore the plural is formed with "au" instead of "eu." The diphthong "ei" is used much more frequently than the diphthong "ai" If you do not know which of the two to use, use the "ei," because the probability of getting it right is significantly higher. The "ie" is pronounced as a long "i." Again, it is difficult to know when it is a simple "I," and when it is an "ie."

Diphthong pronunciation examples:

EI/AI - as the English "I" - **I**ron/M**y**

IE – as the "e" in English – F**ee**l

EU/ÄU - similar to the "oi" in "to boil"

AU - similar to the "ou" in "to bounce"

Ss or β?

The ß (Esszett) is formed from a double "s"; it is a so-called "voiceless s." The Eßzett is used only after a long vowel, if one must consider whether one must use a double "s." For example, a sharp "s" is not used for "Lesen (read)" or "Rasen (lawn)." Unfortunately, there is no simple rule with which you can learn when to use the ß and when the ss. But the words with ß are limited. As long as you memorize them, you will be successful.

Here are a few common examples:

Spaß   - fun

Straße - street

Gruß - greeting

Floß - raft

Heißen - be called

Groß - big

The "sch" and "ch"

The "ch" does not really exist in English. There are two different ways that Germans pronounce the "ch." The "sch" is almost always pronounced the same. The only exception is the letter sequence "ssch," which is pronounced as a double "s" and "ch" separated.

Ch - after "a, o, u, au" – in the back of the mouth – Bach

Ch - after "e, i, eu, ei, ä, ö, ü, äu, ai", or consonant like the "h" in "huge" – Fichte

Sch - always the same, (exception "ssch" (bisschen)) - like the "sh" in English

Letter case

German is not hard to learn. You just need to remember that all nouns and names are capitalized. Verbs and adjectives, as well as pronouns and conjugations, are lower case. As you have already noticed in this chapter, every word at the beginning of the sentence is capitalized after a point.

Summary

After completing this part, you should be able to spell your name. If a "ch" or "sch" occurs in your name, you now know how to pronounce it in German!

Exercises

1. Find and highlight the words containing "ch," which is pronounced like the "h" in "huge".

Heute Morgen bin ich um elf aufgewacht. Ich hatte Pech, denn ich habe den Wecker nicht gehört. Heute werde ich einfach zuHause bleiben. Vielleicht kann ich auch einen Film sehen. Es ist in Ordnung, wenn man sich ein bisschen von allem erholen will. Morgen ist wieder ein neuer Tag. Mein Vater holt mich ab und wir werden in einen Wald voller Fichten gehen. Vielleicht werden wir auch meine Schwester mitnehmen.

2. Insert the correct word from the parenthesis into the space.

a) _____ (Eulen/Äulen) sind sehr interessante Tiere.

b) Hier gibt es viele _____ (Heuser/Häuser).

c) Im _____ (Mei/Mai) hat _____ (meine/maine) Mutter Geburtstag.

d) Am Freitag _____ (flige/fliege) ich nach Italien.

e) Es ist wirklich _____ (heiß/haiß) draußen.

3. Insert the correct word.

a) Der _____ (Hund/hund) muss zum Tierarzt.

b) ___ (ich/Ich) bin sehr hungrig.

Hast du heute _____ (deine/Deine) Mutter gesehen?

c) Mein bester _____ (Freund/ freund) hat heute Geburtstag.

d) Hast du ____ (Lust/lust) mit mir spazieren zu gehen?

e) _____ (Heute/heute) ist ein sehr schöner Tag.

Chapter 2 – The basics

Nouns - main words

Mann, Hund, Katze, Maus: Nouns. In German, Nomen (nouns; also called "Hauptwort") is a word category. It refers to living beings, things, or facts. Nouns in German are always capitalized. In this chapter, you'll learn everything you need to know about nouns.

Why do I recognize the gender of a noun? That will determine which of the three common German articles (der, die, das) you have to use, which is a bit confusing for everyone who learns German as a foreign language.

How to form the plural of a noun? What is the plural of mouse? Mause or Mäuse?

What are the "4 cases" of the noun? And how do you recognize them?

After finishing this chapter, you should be able to answer all these questions!

Forming the plural

Once you have more than one of one thing, it is considered plural and no longer singular. In German, there are eight different plural formations.

Plural formation of nouns

Plural endings

-e der Fisch/die Fische

Umlaut + e die Sau/ die Säue

-n die Blume/ die Blumen

-er das Bild/die Bilder

Umlaut + er das Blatt/die Blätter

No change der Flieger/ die Flieger

Umlaut changes der Garten/ die Gärten

-s das Auto/die Autos

When learning the German language, it is easier if you learn the plural of nouns right away. For many nouns, there are rules that help form plurals. Note that for some nouns there is no plural form; the singular form is used for both. An example of this is tiger, which remains the same in both the singular and the plural forms.

Gender	Ending	Plural	Example
Masculine/Neuter	-el, -er, -en	same as the singular	der Lehrer/die Lehrer
Masculine with one syllable		-e, or umlaut+e	der Block/die Blöcke der Hund/die Hünde
Neutral with one syllable		-er, or umlaut + er	das Kind/die Kinder das Blatt/die Blätter
Feminine	-el	-n	die Fabel/die Fabeln
Feminine with one syllable		-en or umlaut + e	die Frau/die Frauen die Kuh/die Kühe
All	-e	-n	die Farbe/die Farben
All	-o, -a, -i, -u	-s	die Oma/die Omas

These rules are the same for most nouns, but there are always a few exceptions. When dealing with the monosyllable nouns, sometimes you have to determine if an umlaut needs to be used.

Some words do not have a plural form.

Material designations: die Milch, das Fleisch, das Wasser, das Silber…

Collective terms: das Publikum, das Gemüse, das Obst, das Gepäck…

Names of cities, rivers, countries

Abstract terms: die Jugend, die Kindheit. Die Kälte, die Wärme…

While there are some rules for forming the plurals of German words, they cannot be applied to all nouns. The best way is to learn the plural of nouns directly with the singular forms.

Masculine, feminine, neuter

A noun can either be masculine (der), feminine (die), or neuter (das). In this chapter, you will learn which noun belongs to which gender. However, as always in the German language, there are a few exceptions.

Masculine:

1. The natural gender: der Vater, der Onkel, der Opa, der Sohn …

2. Professions: der Koch, der Arzt, der Lehrer, der Verkäufer…

3. Seasons: der Frühling, der Winter, der Herbst, der Sommer…

4. Months: der Dezember, der Februar, der Januar…

5. Most nouns ending with the following letters:

ant – der Lieferant, der Diamant …

är – der Bär, der Milliardär, der Veterinär

eur – der Kommandeur, der Friseur, der Operateur …

ich – der Bereich, der Teich …

ig – der Teig, der Hönig, der König …

iker – der Grafiker, der Musiker, der Klassiker …

ist – der Finalist, der Speziaist, der Geist …

ling – der Liebling, der Fremdling, der Flüchtling …

or – der Prozessor, der Senior, der Gladiator …

Feminine:

1. The natural gender: die Mutter, die Schwester, die Oma …

2. Numbers: die eins, die zwei, die drei …

3. Most trees: die Tanne, die Kiefer, die Eiche … (exception: der Ahorn)

4. Flowers: die Rose, die Tulpe, die Sonnenblume ...

5. Most nouns ending with the following letters:

ei – die Schieberei, die Bekerei, die Malerei ...

in - die Asiatin, die Lehrerin...

keit – die Kurzlebigkeit, die Ähnlichkeit, die Müdigkeit ...

ung- die Umgebung, die Lösung, die Wendung...

ion – die Auktion, die Funktion...

ine – die Maschine, die, die Praline, die Violine ...

schaft- die Gemeinschaft, die Freundschaft, die Mitgliedschaft...

ade – die Olympiade, die Fasade ...

ette – die Facette, die Kette, die Plakette ...

ik – die Politik, die Elektrik, die Grafik ...

ur – die Arhitektur, die Prozedur, die Figur ...

sis – die Analysis, die Basis, die Synthesis

tät – die Realität, die Spezialität

heit – die Freiheit, die Blödheit, die Schöhnheit ...

ie – die Phobie, die Chemie, die Melodie ...

Neuter: Neutral nouns

Most nouns ending with the following letters:

chen- das Mädchen, das Kämmchen ...

lein – das Spieglein, das Blümlein ...

tum – das Datum, das Wachstum ...

o – das Foto, das Radio ...

ett – das Bett, das Fett, das Omlett ...

ment – das Kompliment, das Element ...

ma – das Thema, das Schema, das Klima ...

um – das Zentrum, das Album ...

Nominative, Accusative, Genitive, Dative

These are called the four cases in German. An overview of the cases is very important in German because it is only way to recognize which sentence member is a noun. Otherwise, you can't understand long and complicated sentences. To find out which sentence member is your noun, you only need to ask the following W questions:

Nominative: According to the nominative, you can ask "wer oder was (who or what)?". (Ex: Wer oder was liegt auf dem Tisch? (Who or what is on the table?))

Accusative: According to the accusative, you can ask "wen oder was (who or what)?". (Ex: Wen oder was hast du gesehen? (Who or what did you see?))

Genitive: According to the genitive, you can ask "wessen (whose)?". (Ex: wessen Stift ist das? (Whose pen is this?))

Dative: According to the dative, you can ask "wem (whom)?". (Ex: mit wem gehst du zur Schule? (With whom will you go to the school?))

Table of four cases in the singular

	Nominative	Accusative	Genitive	Dative
Masculine	der Vater	des Vaters	dem Vater	den Vater
Feminine	die Blume	der Blume	der Blume	der Blume
Neuter	das Wasser	des Wassers	dem Wasser	das Wasser

Sample sentences:

Der Vater gießt die Blume.

„der Vater" steht hier im Nominativ: Wer oder was gießt die Blume? - der Vater

"Die Blume" ist in diesem Satz im Akkusativ: Wen oder was gießt der Vater? - die Blume

Das Wasser dient der Blume.

"Blume" steht hier im Dativ: Wem dient das Wasser? – der Blume

"Das Wasser" steht hier im Nominativ: Wer oder was dient der Blume? - das Wasser

Die Blume der Frau.

"der Frau" im Genitiv: Wessen Blume ist das? - der Frau

"Die Blume" steht hier im Nominativ: Wer oder was gehört Frau? - die Blume

Table of four cases in the plural

	Nominative	Genitive	Accusative	Dative
Masculine	die Fehler	der Fehler	den Fehlern	die Fehler
Feminine	die Schule	der Schulen	den Schulen	die Schulen
Neuter	die Kinder	der Kinder	den Kindern	die Kinder

As you can see, the four cases in the plural are much easier to learn. This is because you always use the article "die" in the plural, so you only have to learn one of the lines to know how to use the four cases for all three genders.

Exercises

1. In the postcard below, select all subjects that are in nominative.

Hallo Alisa!

Meine Famillie und ich haben hier in Spanien viel Spaß. Das Wetter ist einfach fantastisch. Wie geht es mit den Prüfungen? Hast du irgendwelche interessante Neuigkeiten? Unser Onkel kommt uns vielleicht sogar hier besuchen. Er hat sich die nächste Woche frei genommen. Die Umgebung ist wirklich toll. Du solltest uns auch besuchen!

Liebe Grüße

Marie

2. Mark all nouns with articles in the plural form.

Hallo Anna!

Ich war gestern bei meiner Freundin Lena. Sie hat viele Hunde und sogar eine Katze. Ich liebe Tiere und besonders Hunde. Ich habe auch ihre Schwestern kennengelernt. Der Tag war sehr schön. Morgen werden wir zusammen ins Kino gehen. Die Filme die im Angebot sind, sehen alle cool aus. Wir wissen immer noch nicht welchen wir schauen werden.

Ich hoffe dir geht es gut.

Liebe Grüße

Sarah

3. Fill in the spaces with the appropriate article. (masculine - der, feminine - die, neuter - das)

____ Zimmer ist wirklich schön.

Ich habe vergessen ____ Tür zu schließen.

____ Kaffeemaschine funktioniert ausgezeichnet.

Hast du ____ Foto von unserem Urlaub gesehen?

____ Hund ist krank.

____ Opa von Lena besucht uns Heute.

Chapter 3 – Pronouns

What are pronouns?

Pronouns are words which serve to replace nouns in a sentence. There are different types of pronouns which fulfill different tasks. In this chapter, you will learn the types of pronouns and how they are used.

Overview of German pronouns

Personal pronouns

Personal pronouns, like all other pronouns, are used to replace nouns and thus avoid repetitions. In their normal form (ich, du, er, sie, es, wir, ihr, sie), the personal pronouns are in the nominative. However, they can be declined in the dative (e.g., ich → mir) and accusative (e.g., ich → mich).

Example: Ich sitze auf dem Grass. Mir gefällt die Natur. Ich entspanne mich.

Possessive pronouns

Possessive pronouns show ownership. There are two types of possessive pronouns: the possessive pronoun as a companion and the possessive pronoun as a substitute.

Example: Das ist mein Hund. (Companion) – Das ist mein. (Substitute)

Reflexive pronouns

Reflexive pronouns refer to subjects. The reflexive pronouns are used when the subject and the object have the same person in a sentence.

Example: Ich wasche mich. (With reflexive verb) – Wir kennen uns. (With reciprocal verb)

Relative pronouns

Relative pronouns introduce relative clauses. There are determining relative clauses, which are necessary for the understanding of the sentence, and non-determining relative clauses, which contain additional information. In German, there are different relative pronouns depending on the case.

Example: Gestern habe ich meinen Hund zum Tierarzt gebracht, welche von einem Auto angefahren wurde.

Demonstrative pronouns

Demonstrative pronouns are used to make statements about people, things, or places, or to make excerpts in one sentence. In German, there are several demonstrative pronouns, each of which is used for a different purpose (e.g.diese, jene).

Example: Ich hätte gerne diese Farbe.

Indefinite pronouns

Indefinite pronouns are used to generalize facts. They include, for example, something or someone (etwas, jemand).

Example: Kannst du mir etwas bringen?

Interrogative pronouns

Interrogative pronouns are used to replace a noun after which something is asked. In German, there are the following interrogative pronouns: who, what, whom, whom, whose (wer, was, wem, wen, wessen).

Example: Wem gehört diese Tasche?

What are personal pronouns?

Personal pronouns replace the nouns in a sentence. However, in most cases, they are not capitalized (exception: courtesy form; more on this later).

Singular (1) and Plural (2)

1st person: ich (1) – wir (2)

2nd person: du (1) ihr (2)

3rd person: er, sie, es (1) sie (2)

Most German personal pronouns are used in exactly the same way as in English.

Personal pronouns

ich = I

du, Sie = you

er, sie, es = he, she, it

wir = we

ihr, Sie = you

sie = they

The biggest difference is that in German, the form "Sie" is in the second person singular and plural. The "Sie" form is also called courtesy form.

When do you use "du" and when "Sie"?

At first, nobody will be offended when you mix the two forms, so do not worry! Simply speaking, one uses the courtesy form when one does not know the person to which they are speaking. When you want to be polite, the initial letter is always capitalized; do not confuse the "Sie" with the "sie." Also, do not approach the person with their first name, but with the surname (Mr. Mueller, Mrs. Meier).

Examples include:

your teachers

your doctor

the cashier in the supermarket

the grandparents of your friends

the police.

The courtesy form is especially important to elderly people in Germany, so if you help an older lady across the street, you should address her with "Sie."

The "du" form in German can be used to address friends, family, or children. It also depends on the environment in which you meet someone. For example, you should introduce yourself directly with your first name at work, but wait and see what the person you speak to will say. If he only tells you his first name, you can assume that he wants you to tell him your first name. If you are not sure, use the courtesy form.

Declination of personal pronouns

	1.Person Sg.	2.Person Sg.		3.Person Sg.		1.Person Pl.	2.Person Pl.	3.Person Pl.
Nom.	Ich	du/Sie	Er	Sie	es	wir	ihr/Sie	sie
Gen.	Meiner	deiner/Ihrer	seiner	Ihrer	seiner	unser	euer/Ihr	ihrer
Dat.	Mir	dir/Ihnen	ihm	Ihr	ihm	uns	euch/Ihnen	ihnen
Acc.	Mich	dich/Sie	ihn	Sie	es	uns	euch/Sie	sie

Examples: courtesy form personal pronouns

"Ich bringe Ihnen eine Gabel!" (Courtesy form)

"Können Sie mir bitte die Gabel reichen?" (Courtesy form)

"Ich freue mich dich wieder zu sehen!" (Du-form)

"Ich habe es Ihnen Gestern gesagt!" (Courtesy form)

"Wie geht es dir?" (Du-form)

"Hast du Hunger?" (Du-form)

"Haben Sie die Tests korrigiert?" (Courtesy form)

"Ich habe dich durch das Fenster gesehen!" (Du-form)

Exercise

1. Add the correct personal pronoun in each sentence below. Pay attention to the case of each pronoun.

a) Hallo Anna. Hast ___ Lena gesehen? ___ habe heute schon den ganzen Tag Durst.

b) Hallo Frau Müller! Wie geht es ____? Ich hoffe ____ beiden geht es gut.

c) Hallo Maria. Wie geht es ___?

d) Hallo Frau Schmidt, hallo Herr Schmidt, haben ____ meinen Hund gesehen?

e) Ja Papa, ___ geht es gut. Wie geht es ___?

f) Hast du heute schon was von Anna gehört? - Nein, ___ hat mich heute noch nicht angerufen.

What are possessive pronouns?

Possessive pronouns are possession-indicating pronouns. They state who owns something or to whom something belongs (possession / affiliation). They are declined, and their gender adapts exactly to singular or plural according to the corresponding noun. Possessive pronouns have two different functions.

You can represent a companion of a noun. (Das ist mein Stift.)

You can replace a noun if the noun has been mentioned before. (Wem gehört der Stift? – Das ist meiner.)

Declination possessive pronoun (as companion):

Nominative

	ich	du	Er	Sie	Es	wir	ihr	sie
Masculine/ Neuter	mein	dein	Sein	Ihr	Sein	unser	euer	ihr
Feminine/ Plural	meine	deine	seine	Ihre	seine	unsere	eure	ihre

Genitive

	ich	du	Er	Sie	Es	wir	ihr	sie
Masculine/ Neuter	meines	deines	seines	ihres	seines	unseres	eures	ihres
Feminine/ Plural	meiner	deiner	seiner	ihrer	seiner	unserer	eurer	ihrer

Dative

	ich	du	Er	sie	es	wir	ihr	sie
Masculine/Neuter	meinem	deinem	seinem	ihrem	seinem	unserem	eurem	ihrem
Feminine	meiner	Deiner	seiner	ihrer	seiner	unserer	eurer	ihrer
Plural	meinen	Deinen	seinen	ihren	seinen	unseren	euren	ihren

Accusative

	ich	du	Er	Sie	es	wir	ihr	sie
Masculine	meinen	deinen	seinen	ihren	seinen	unseren	euren	ihren
Neuter	mein	dein	Sein	Ihr	sein	unser	euer	ihr
Feminine / Plural	meine	deine	seine	Ihre	seine	unsere	eure	ihre

Declination possessive pronoun (as a substitute for a noun):

Nominative

	ich	du	Er	Sie	es	wir	ihr	sie
Masculine	meiner	deiner	seiner	ihrer	seiner	unserer	eurer	ihrer
Neuter	meins	deins	seins	ihres	seins	unseres	eures	ihres
Feminine / Plural	meine	deine	seine	Ihre	seine	unsere	eure	ihre

Genitive

	ich	du	Er	Sie	es	wir	ihr	sie
Masculine / Neuter	meines	deines	seines	ihres	seines	unseres	eures	ihres
Feminine / Plural	meiner	deiner	seiner	ihrer	seiner	unserer	eurer	ihrer

Examples with possessive pronouns (as companion):

Hast du deine Sonnenbrille dabei?

Es hat seine Sonnenbrille im Haus vergessen.

Sie hat ihre Sonnenbrille dabei.

Das ist die Cousine meiner Freundin.

Hast du seine Katze gesehen?

Deine Katze ist süß.

Ist das nicht dein Buch?

Ich habe meiner Mutter gesagt, dass ich später komme.

Examples with possessive pronouns (as a substitute for a noun):

Wem gehört der Stift? – Das ist meiner.

Wessen Auto ist das? - Meins.

Meine Tochter ist 12 Jahre alt. – Meine ist erst 6.

Hast du auch deinen Hung mitgebracht? – Nein, ich habe meinen im Haus gelasen.

Wo ist eurer?

Meine Hunde sind oft im Haus, und eure?

Wessen Shuche sind das? – Das sind ihre.

Exercise

1. Insert the correct possessive pronoun. The first sentence gives you an example.

*Ich habe meine (ich) Tasche vergessen.

a) Hast du ____ (du) Buch dabei? - Ich habe _____ (ich) vergessen.

b) Wie geht es _____ (du) Vater?

c) Wem gehört der Wagen? - Das ist _____ (er).

d) Hat sie ____ (sie) Freund noch?

e) Ich habe mir ein neues Kleid gekauft. - Hast du ____ (du) altes immer noch?

f) Du bist _____ (er) erste Freundin.

What are relative pronouns?

The German relative pronouns are der, die, das oder welcher, welche, and welches. One can either use the pronouns "der, die, das," or "welcher, welche, welches." They introduce relative clauses, which are subsidiary clauses. They describe something more closely. The gender, the number, and the case of the relative pronoun are dependent on its reference word.

Declination relative pronouns:

	Nominative	Accusative	Genitive	Dative
Masculine	der, welcher	Dessen	dem, welchem	den, welchen
Feminine	die, welche	Deren	der, welcher	die, welche
Neuter	das, welches	Dessen	dem, welchem	das, welches
Plural	die, welche	Deren	denen, welchen	die, welche

Examples of relative pronouns:

Der Mann, den ich Gestern gesehen habe.

Der Mann, welchen ich gestern gesehen habe.

Die Frau, die immer Jeans trägt.

Die Frau, welche immer Jeans trägt.

Das Haus, das eine schöne Farbe hat.

Das Haus, welches eine schöne Farbe.

Ich habe einen Computer gesehen, den ich schon immer kaufen wollte.

Hast du immer noch den Stift, den ich dir gegeben habe?

Das ist der Mann, dessen Frau im Krankenhaus arbeitet.

Hier sind die Kinder, die im Park spielen

Exercise

1. Add the correct form of the relative pronoun.

a) Die Stadt, ____ ich gesehen habe, war schön.

b) Hast du den Kuchen gegessen, ____ ich gestern gebacken habe?

c) Hast du den Mann heute gesehen, ____ dich komisch angesehen hat?

d) Ich habe meine Hasuaufgaben schon alle gemacht, ____ ich heute aufbekommen habe.

e) Ich habe heute die Frau getroffen, ____ Katze weggelaufen ist.

What are reflexive pronouns?

The reflexive pronoun refers back to the subject. The reflexive pronouns are a complement to reflexive verbs and reciprocal verbs. The reflexive verb refers to a subject (Example: Ich wasche mich.). The reciprocal verb can only be plural. It expresses a reciprocal relationship between several subjects and objects (Example: Anna und Mario streiten sich jeden Tag.).

	1.person Sg.	2.person Sg.	3.person Sg.	1.person Pl.	2.person Pl.	3.person Pl.
Dative	mir	dir	sich	Uns	euch	sich
Accusative	mich	dich	sich	Uns	euch	sich

List of reflexive verbs:

In the following list you will find some of the German relative verbs that you use with the relative pronouns.

Reflexive verbs with reflexive pronouns	Example
sich ausruhen	Ich ruhe mich aus
sich erkälten	Du hast dich erkältet
sich schämen	Er schämt sich
sich wundern	Sie wundert sich
sich erholen	Wir erholen uns
sich kümmern	Ihr kümmert euch
sich bedanken	Sie bedanken sich
sich beeilen	Du beeilst dich
sich bemühen	Er bemüht sich
sich vorstellen	Sie stellt sich was vor

sich irren	Ich irre mich
sich weigern	Ihr weigert euch

Exercise

1. Add the right reflexive pronouns into the gaps.

a) Sie wäscht ____.

b) Wir ruhen ____ aus.

c) Sie schämen ____.

D) Ich habe ____ meinem Chef vorgestellt.

e) Sie kümmert ____ um sie.

f) Ihr habt ____ geirrt.

What are demonstrative pronouns?

Demonstrative pronouns are indicative. These pronouns can be used in two different ways- as article words (Example: Dieser Hund ist sehr süß) or to represent the noun in a sentence (Example: Dieser [Mädchen zeigt auf einen Hund, spricht das Wort Hund aber nicht aus] ist sehr süß).

jener, jene, jenes (gleiche Bedeutung wie der da, oder der dort)

dieser, diese, dieses

der da, die da, das daDemonstrativpronomen

dieser dort, diese dort, dieses dort

derjenige, diejenige(n), dasjenige

derselbe, dieselbe, dasselbe

der, die, da

Declination demonstrative pronouns:

	Nominative	Genitive	Accusative	Dative
Masculine	dieser/jener	dieses/jenes	diesem/jenem	diesen/jenen
Feminine	diese/jene	dieser/jener	dieser/jener	diese/jene
Neuter	dieses/jenes	dieses/jenes	diesem/jenem	dieses/jenes

	Nominative	Genitive	Accusative	Dative
Masc.	derjenige/derselbe	desselben/desjenigen	Demselben/demjenigen	denselben/denjenigen
Fem.	diejenige/dieselbe	derselben/derjenigen	derselben/derjenigen	dieselbe/diejenigen
Neut.	dasjenige/dasselbe	desselben/desjenigen	demselben/demjenigen	dasselbe/dasjenige

Examples of demonstrative pronouns:

Derjenige, der als erstes das Buch liest, bekommt eine höhere Note.

Ich gehe auf dieselbe Schule wie du.

Welchen Ball findest du am besten? - Den da.

Welche Katze gefällt dir? - Diese.

Was für eine Lampe ist das? Dieselbe, die du gestern gekauft hast.

Dasselbe oder das gleiche?

"Dasselbe" is not synonymous for "das gleiche," but many Germans make this mistake. "Dasselbe" is used when talking about one unique thing.

An example of "dasselbe": Anna hat sich bei ihrer Freundin ein Buch über Hunde ausgeliehen, dasselbe Buch hat Maria sich vor 3 Monaten ausgeliehen. (This is the one and the same book, which first Maria and then Anna has borrowed.)

An example of "das gleiche": Lena hat sich ein neues Kleid gekauft. Als sie sich mit Anna getroffen hat, sagte sie: "Ich habe das gleiche Kleid." Anna can not have "dasselb,"; she can only have "das gleiche," because "dasselbe" is referring to only one unique thing. For this reason, it can't hang in Anna's wardrobe.

Exercise

1. Select all demonstrative pronouns in the text. (Both the demonstrative pronouns accompanying a noun and those that replace a noun)

Diese Katze ist so süß! - Wirklich? Ich finde diese dort besser. Der Kühlschrank ist leer. - Kein Problem, ich kann einkaufen gehen. Welchen Kuchen möchtest du? - Denjenigen, den ich vor einer Woche gekauft habe. Hast du einen neuen Freund? - Nein, immer noch derselbe. Mit diesen Klamotten willst du joggen gehen? Die sind doch gar nicht bequem!

What are indefinite pronouns?

Indefinite pronouns are indeterminate. They are used in German to generalize something (for example, Das kann man nicht so machen.). Some indefinite pronouns refer to a whole set, like "alles" or "jeder," some of them refer to a subset, such as "manche or einige," and others refer to people or things, such as "jeder, etwas oder jeder."

Indefinite pronoun list

Person	Example	Things	Example	Person and Things	Example
Man	Man kann das nicht genau sagen.	etwas	Von dem Essen ist noch etwas übrig.	alle	Alle wollten ins Kino gehen.
Jemand	Hat jemand meinen Hund gesehen?	nichts	Es ist nichts mehr übrig.	einige	Einige von ihnen kamen nicht.
Niemand	Niemand hat das gemacht.	alles	Das haben wir alles schon gemacht.	jeder	Nicht jeder von uns kann das.
		welcher	Gibt es noch Käse? – Ja, im Kühlschrank ist noch welcher.	ein	Ich habe Karten. Willst du eine?
		ein bisschen	Ein bisschen gibt es noch.	kein	Ich möchte keine.
		ein wenig	Ein wenig ist noch da.	manch-	Für manche Sachen musst du Talent haben.
		meiste	Das meiste wurde schon gegessen.	mehrere	Mehrere sind auf das Konzert gegangen.

Examples with indefinite pronouns for persons:

Waren gestern viele im Kino? - Ja einige.

Manche aus unserer Klasse können sehr gut Deutsch.

Man braucht nicht viel zu gehen.

Jeder hier muss sich erholen.

Alle kennen diese Lektion.

Einer hat gestern aufs Konzert gegangen.

Mehrere sind gestern nicht gekommen.

Examples with indefinite pronouns for things:

Ich habe etwas für dich.

Was machst du heute? - Einiges, spazieren, ausgehen...

In der Küche ist noch ein bisschen Kuchen, aber das meiste ist schon gegessen.

Hast du Durst? - Ja, ein wenig.

Declination of the most important indefinite pronouns:

Nominative	Dative	Accusative
niemand	Niemandem	niemanden
jemand	Jemandem	jemanden
jeder	Jedem	jeden
jede	Jeder	jede
jedes	Jedem	jedes

Indefinite pronoun man

The "man" in German has nothing to do with the noun "Mann." The indefinite pronoun is a general person. There is no translation in English that has exactly the same meaning. The pronoun responds to every possible person. The "man" is like a person X.

Nominative	Dative	Accusative
man	Einem	einen

Examples with man:

Man muss nur viel Motivation haben. (Wer oder was muss Motivation haben?)

Die laute Musik geht einem auf die Nerven! (Wem geht die Musik auf die Nerven?)

Der Stau stört einen wirklich. (Wen oder was stört der Stau?)

Exercise

1. Add the right form of "man" to the sentences below. (man, einen, einem). Tip: Always ask the W questions to find out which form is the right one.

a) Was kann ___ denn noch sagen?

b) Da läuft ___ ja das Wasser im Mund zusammen.

c) Kann ___ den Kaffee schon trinken oder ist er noch zu heiß?

d) Darf ___ im Krankenhaus das Handy benutzen?

e) Das geht ___ ziemlich auf die Nerven.

f) Du machst ___ ein ganz schlechtes Gewissen.

What are interrogative pronouns?

You have already encountered interrogative pronouns here in the chapter on sentence construction. With these pronouns you can ask for something. Interrogative pronouns are question words. In questions with interrogative pronouns, the pronouns replace the noun. The pronoun "was für ein" is used to ask for a kind or category. For example, if you want to ask for the kind of a dog: Was für ein Hund ist das? - A Labrador.

Examples of interrogative pronouns:

Interrogative pronoun	Example
Wer	Wer ist das?
Was	Was machst du?
Wem	Wem gehört das?
Wen	Wen hast du gesehen?
Wessen	Wessen Kleid ist das?
Welcher	Welcher Ball ist gelb?
Was für ein	Was für ein Hund ist das?

Exercise

1. Add the correct interrogative pronouns into the spaces below.

a) _____ gehört der Ball?

b) _____ Hund ist das? (asking about the kind of the dog)

c) _____ habe ich mein Buch geliehen?

d) _____ hast du angerufen?

e) _____ (Hut) gehört dir?

The specific article

You use the specific article in German if you speak about something specific (for example, if you point at something). There are three specific articles in German – der, die, and das. These three articles vary according to the gender of the noun that follows. In the chapter about nouns, you learned that a noun is either masculine, feminine, or neutral. The following table shows the relationship between the gender of a noun and an article in the singular form. In the plural form, article determination is much simpler and will be discussed later.

Gender of the noun	Nominative	Genitive	Dative	Accusative
Masculine	der	des	dem	den
Feminine	die	der	der	die
Neuter	das	des	Dem	das

Der, die, das rules:

If you have a noun in the masculine, then you use the article: DER

If you have a noun in the feminine, then you use the article: DIE

If you have a noun in the neuter, then you use the article: DAS

The specific article in the plural

As already mentioned, the use of the German article in the plural is much simpler. For the plural, the article is always "die," no matter which gender the noun has.

Gender of the noun	Nominative	Genitive	Dative	Accusative
Masculine	die	der	den	die
Feminine	die	der	den	die
Neuter	die	der	den	die

Examples for the specific article:

Das ist mein Kleid. (The woman shows exactly which dress.)

Der Hund von Anna hat der ganzen Tag geschlafen. (Anna has only one dog.)

Der Bruder von meinem Freund ist wirklich schlau. (The girl has only one boyfriend.)

Das Auto von meinem Freund ist neu. (The friend has only one car.)

The undefined article

You use the undefined article in German when talking about a category / group of something. The undefined article (ein, eine) is only in the singular; in the plural, it is mostly omitted (for example, "Da liegen Orangen") or used for a quantity indication (for example, "Kannst du mir zwei Organgen geben"). The undefined article "eine" is used before nouns that are feminine; neuter or masculine nouns use "ein."

Gender of the noun	Nominative	Genitive	Dative	Accusative
Masculine	ein	eines	einem	einen
Feminine	eine	einer	einer	eine
Neuter	ein	eines	einem	ein

Examples for the undefined article:

Ich möchte eine Orange. (From the box in which there are several oranges)

Kannst du mit einen Apfel geben? (From the box in which there are many apples)

Gib mit bitte ein Stück Kuchen. (From a big cake)

Negative articles

In German, as in almost every language, there is a negative article, which denies that something is present. Consider the following example: "Es gibt kein Kuchen mehr." This sentence denies that there is any cake.

Gender of the noun	Article	Example
Masculine	kein	kein Brot
Feminine	keine	keine Marmelade
Neuter	kein	kein Auto

Now you know the most important things about German articles. Our tip for you: Learn each noun directly with the article, because the German language is full of exceptions, and this approach will certainly help you to use the articles correctly.

Exercise

1. Insert the correct undefined or specific article below.

a) Ich möchte mir _____ neues Kleid kaufen.

b) _____ ist mein neues Auto!

c) Gehört _____ Hund dir?

d) _____ ist meine Katze.

e) _____ Wetter ist heute sehr schlecht.

f) _____ Tag pro Woche nehme ich mir nichts vor.

g) _____ Junge, von dem ich dir gestern erzählt habe.

Chapter 4 – Sentence construction

Depending on which sentence types you use, you have to put the different sentence members into their properorder. A distinction is made between questions and other sentences. Furthermore, there is a distinction between main etches and secondary theorems.

Recognize the members

Subject: the subject is always a noun or pronoun, which is in the nominative (e.g., der Hund, das Haus)

Predicate: the predicate is a conjugated verb (e.g., [er] läuft, [sie] fährt, [ich] tanze)

Object: the object is like the subject, a noun or pronoun

Adverbial determination: the adverbial determination is a propositional term which designates neither the subject, nor the predicate, nor the object (e.g. adverbs, adjectives)

Declarative sentence

Declarative sentences make a claim, an assumption, or a statement about a fact.

1. subject - 2. predicate - 3. object / adverbial determination ...

Anna besucht ihren Vater.

Since the subject is nominative, we find out with the W-question of the nominative what the subject is. Who or what visits their father? Anna - "Anna" is consequently the subject here.

"besucht" is the conjugated verb (sie besucht)

Whom or what does Anna visit? Her father - "ihren Vater" is therefore the object.

Interrogative sentence

In German, there are two different ways to ask a question- with a question word and without a question word.

Question with question word:

In order to explain the question with a question word, you need an overview of the German question words:

Question word	English	Use	Example
Wer	who	subject/person	Wer hat das gemacht?
Was	what	subject or object	Was kann ich da kaufen?
Wen	whom	accusative object, direct object (person)	Wen hast du gesehen?
Wohin	where	place (the direction)	Wohin geht sie?
Womit	whereby/with	forms from "mit" and "was"	Womit habt ihr den Hund gefüttert.
Wie	how	a way	Wie haben Sie das geschafft?
Woran	whereof	forms from "an" and "was"	Woran liegt das?
Wem	whom	dative object, indirect object	Wem gehört der Hund?
Wessen	whose	belonging	Wessen Kleid

Question word	English	Use	Example
			ist das?
Wo	where	Place (position)	Wo bist du gerade?
Woher	from where	Place (origin)	Woher kommen Sie?
Wann	when	Time	Wann kommst du nach Deutschland?
warum/weshalb/wieso	why	reason for doing something	Warum hast du das gemacht?
Wozu	why	aim of doing something	Wozu braucht er das?
welche(r/s)	which	Choice	Welcher Ball gehört dir?

As you can see, the question word is always at the beginning of the sentence. There is also another way to ask a question with a question word; you can put a preposition in front of some question word.

Mit wem warst du gestern im Kino?

Für wen hast du gekocht?

Mit was hast du es gemacht?

An was hast du gedacht?

Question without question word:

Questions without a question word can always be answered with "yes" or "no." The order is as follows:

1. predicate – 2. subject – 3. object / adverbial determination ...

Sample sentences:

Bist du hungrig?

Willst du etwas essen?

Hast du Heute Marcus gesehen?

Geht es dir gut?

In these sentences, there is always a predicate at the beginning and the subject in the second place (who or what is hungry? - du - is in the nominative, so it is the subject).

Main clause and subordinate clause

Of course, not every sentence is as easy to understand as "Anna besucht ihren Vater." This is considered a main sentence. To avoid having to start a new sentence after three words, we use secondary sentences. In German, the sentences are separated by a comma. The main difference between the two types of sentences is that the conjugated verb is placed in the main sentence at the first (interrogative sentence) or the second (declarative sentencet) point. In the subordinate, the conjugated verb is at the end of the sentence. You always recognize the main sentence because it can stand alone. You can cut the subordinate clause and the main sentence still makes sense. This is different with the subordinate sentence. It is dependent on the main sentence and can not stand alone. Secondary sentences are often introduced by conjunctions (binding words).

Conjunction	English	Example
Weil	because	Ich habe die Kleider mitgenommen, weil ich sie brauche.
Wenn	if/when	Ich gehe schlafen, wenn ich die Hausaufgaben erledige.
Dass	that	Ich habe gesehen, dass du gekommen bist.
Ob	whether/if	Du wolltest wissen, ob der Kuchen gut ist.
Als	as	Ich war sehr glücklich, als du mir

		das erzählt hast.
obwohl	although	Der Tag ist schön, obwohl es ein bisschen kalt ist.
nachdem	after	Ich war so sauer, nachdem ich ihn gesehen habe.

The subordinate clause does not have to be at the end of the sentence. It can be at the beginning, and there may also be several minor clauses.

Chapter 5 – German verbs

Verbs describe an activity or condition. Sein (be), warden (to be), können(can), haben(have), sagen(say), sollen(should), geben(give), müssen(have to), gehen(go), and wollen(want) are probably the most frequently used German verbs. We distinguish between regular and irregular verbs. The irregular verbs have to be memorized. In German, there are six different verb tenses.

Present (present)

Preterite (past)

Perfect (past)

Plusquamperfect (past)

Futur 1 (future)

Futur 2 (future)

Verb kinds

In this chapter, you will learn about the most important German verbs and verb forms.

Modal

Reflexive

Passive and active

The verbs "be" and "have"

The imperative

Participles

Some verb forms are used more frequently than others. For example, Germans rarely uses the futur 2, but futur 1 is used very often. In language usage, we also use the preterite and plusquamperfect as often as the perfect. Present, perfect, and future are the most important to learn.

We will use a simple example. Let's say that a chicken practices the German tenses

Present: Ich lege ein Ei= present; in this moment, the chicken lays an egg

Preterite: Ich legte ein Ei= expresses a past act; this form is used more frequently in reports or narrations in written form than in the general language usage

Perfect: Ich habe ein Ei gelegt= expresses an action from the past that has already been completed

Plusquamperfekt: Ich hatte ein Ei gelegt= expresses an action that lies in the past and lies before a certain time

Futur 1: Ich werde ein Ei legen= expresses an action that will be executed in the future; can express a guess about the future.

Futur 2: Ich werde ein Ei gelegt haben= expresses an action that is completed by a certain point in time

Present

The present is the most frequently used tense in the German language. With this form, as the name implies, you can express what happens in the present- Ich backe gerade einen Kuchen. You can also express the future, if the action or the condition is already established- Am Sonntag koche koche ich für meine Freunde.

In addition, the tense expresses actions that are always repeated- Jeden Sonntag koche ich für meine Freunde. Even if you want to say how long something has already taken place, you use the present- Ich koche für meine Freunde jeden Sonntag schon seit 3 Jahren.

Conjugation of German verbs:

Regular verb: lachen (to laugh)

1. person singular: Ich lache - 1. person plural: wir lachen

2. person singular: Du lachst - 2. person plural ihr lacht

3. person singular: er/ sie / es lacht - 3. person plural: sie lachen

Verbs with -e: leiden (to suffer)

1. person singular: Ich leide - 1. person plural: wir leiden

2. person singular: Du leidest - 2. person plural: ihr leidet

3. person singular: er/ sie / es leidet - 3. person plural: sie leiden

Verbs with vowel change: geben (to give)

1. person singular: Ich gebe - 1. person plural: wir geben

2. person singular: Du gibst - 2. person plural: ihr gibt

3. person singular: er/ sie / es gibt - 3. person plural: sie geben

sein (to be)

1. person singular: Ich bin - 1. person plural: wir sind

2. person singular: Du bist - 2. person plural: ihr seid

3. person singular: er/ sie / es ist - 3. person plural: sie sind

haben (to have)

1. person singular: Ich habe - 1. person plural: wir haben

2. person singular: Du hast - 2. person plural: ihr habt

3. person singular: er/ sie / es hat - 3. person plural: sie haben

In the third person, we are given the du-form and the Sie-Form (courtesy form), which in German is usually always written with the second person singular and plural. As you can see, the courtesy form differs from the du-form in the 3rd person plural only by the uppercase "S."

Examples with courtesy in the present

Hallo Herr Müller, Sie haben ein schönes Haus!

Frau Schneider, haben Sie meine Arbeit geprüft?

Herr Fischer, Sie sind sehr nett.

Hallo Herr Richter, warum lachen Sie so selten?

Frau und Herr Schneider, es ist so schön dass Sie hier sind.

Familie Fischer, Sie sind sehr nett!

Exercise

1. Insert the correct ending of the verbs into the spaces below.

a) Er ha_____ ein blaues T-Shirt an.

b) Sie frag_____ nach dem Wetter.

c) Du spiel_____ wirklich gut Tennis!

d) Ha_____ du Lust auf ein Eis?

e) Woll____ ihr mitkommen?

f) Hab_____ ihr schon was vor?

What is the preterite?

As already mentioned, we use the preterite to express the past. However, it is used more frequently in written form than in everyday language. When we speak, we usually use the perfect. If, however, you are reading a narrative story, such as a fairy tale, the preterite will often be used there.

Strong and weak verbs

Before we talk about the formation of the preterite, we must first examine the difference between weak and strong verbs, since these two form the preterite differently.

Weak verbs: They keep their base in the formation of the preterit. Example: legen – Ich legte; only the syllable "te" was added. They also differ in their participle form from the strong verbs, since this always ends with a "t" (gelegt).

Strong verbs: They change their base in the formation of the preterite. Example: lessen – ich las (the "e" becomes an "a"). They also differ in their participle form. This is not always the case, as the verb sitzen – saß - gesessen.

Mixed verbs: Tthey have characteristics of both weak and strong verbs. Example: kennen - kannte - gekannt.

Preterite form

For regular verbs, the following applies:

Weak verbs

Person	Present	Preterite
1.Pers.Sg.	ich sage	ich sag-te
2.Pers.Sg.	du sagst	du sag-test
3.Pers.Sg.	er, sie, es sagt	er,sie,es sag-te
1.Pers.Pl.	wir sagen	wir sag-ten
2.Pers.Pl.	ihr sagt	ihr sag-tet
3.Pers.Pl	sie sagen	sie sag-ten

Strong verbs

Person	Present	Preterite
1.Pers.Sg.	ich esse	ich aß
2.Pers.Sg.	du isst	du aßest
3.Pers.Sg.	er, sie, es isst	er,sie,es aß
1.Pers.Pl.	wir essen	wir aßen
2.Pers.Pl.	ihr esst	ihr aßt
3.Pers.Pl	sie essen	sie aßen

Mixed verbs

Person	Present	Preterite
1.Pers.Sg.	ich bringe	ich brachte
2.Pers.Sg.	du bringst	du brachtest
3.Pers.Sg.	er, sie, es bringt	er,sie,es brachte
1.Pers.Pl.	wir bringen	wir brachten
2.Pers.Pl.	ihr bringt	ihr brachtet
3.Pers.Pl	sie bringen	sie brachten

Modal verbs in the preterite

Modal verbs have an influence on the verb behind it (which is always in the infinitive at the end of the sentence). Example: Ich kann sehr gut lesen.

können – ich kann – ich konnte

dürfen - ich darf - ich durfte

sollen - ich soll - ich sollte

wollen - ich will - ich wollte

mögen - ich mag - ich mochte

müssen - ich muss - ich musste

Example sentences in the preterite:

Ich saß heute auf der Bank neben der Schule. Wo warst du heute?

Er aß gestern den ganzen Kuchen.

Wir sollten alles bis morgen fertig haben.

Ihr musstet sehr weit gehen.

Sie konnte gestern nicht zur Schule kommen.

Ich lag heute den ganzen Tag im Bett.

Du sagtest doch, du würdest kommen.

Exercise

1. Fill in the spaces with the correctt preterite form.

Weak verbs:

Gestern _____(kaufen) ich für die ganze Woche ein.

Er _____(fragen) seine Mutter, ob er ausgehen darf.

Wir _____(sagen), dass wir zu spät kommen würden.

Strong verbs:

Er _____(bitten) mich um Hilfe.

Die Mütter _____ (finden) ihre Kinder auf dem Spielplatz.

Deine Musik _____ (klingen) sehr gut!

The Perfect

In order to speak German perfectly, you have to know everything about the perfect verb form. Germans use the perfect form more often than the preterite, especially in the colloquial language. It is a common way to express the past.

Forming the perfect

To form the German perfect, you need to have a form of "have" or "to be" and the participle II.

Person	to have	Partizip II	Person	to be	Partizip II
Ich	Habe	getanzt	ich	bin	gelaufen
Du	Hast	getanzt	du	bist	gelaufen
er/sie/es	Hat	getanzt	er/sie/es	ist	gelaufen

Wir	Haben	getanzt	wir	sind	gelaufen
Ihr	Habt	getanzt	ihr	seid	gelaufen
Sie	Haben	getanzt	sie	sind	gelaufen

When do you use "sein" and when "haben?"

Sein is used for intransitive verbs to show the following: 1. a state change (Ich bin eingeschlafen [was awake-slept in]), or 2. a change in location (Ich bin gereist). It is always used in the verbs "reisen and gehen, bleiben and geschehen."

Haben is used much more frequently than the verb sein in order to form the perfect. In German, we do not distinguish between words of movement and words that express no movement.

Sample sentences in the perfect:

Ich habe heute Reis gegessen.

Du bist zur Schule gelaufen.

Wir haben zusammen getanzt.

Sie sind ins Hotel gegangen.

Sie haben mich nicht gehört.

Du bist einfach eingeschlafen.

Ihr seid bis 10 Uhr geblieben.

Es ist geschehen.

Sie hat mich gerufen.

Exercise

1. Insert the correct conjugated perfect form of the verb (sein or haben + partizip 2). Here is an example:

Ich habe (haben) gelacht (lachen).

a) Du ___(sein) _____(schwimmen).

b) Maria_____(sein) _____(laufen).

c) Anna und Marcus_____(haben) _____(fragen).

d) Sie und ich _____(haben) _____(weinen).

e) Ihr _____(haben) auf dem Stuhl _____(sitzen).

f) Anna und Lena _____(sein) _____(reisen).

Future 1 and 2

In German, there is the present verb form, which expresses the present but can also describe the future, especially in the colloquial language (Morgen gehe ich früher zur Stadt). There are two verb forms to express the future-future 1 and future 2. Which futur you use depends on what kind of action in the future you want to express.

Future 1: Use if you give a forecast / guess for the future or the present (Am Sonntag wird die Sonne scheinen.). Also, if you are talking about plans in the future (Im Sommer werde ich in den Urlaub gehen.). Furthermore, you use the futur 1 if you make a promise (Ab heute werde ich gesünder essen.).

Future 2: You use future 2 when you predict something that will be completed in the future (Um 3 Uhr werde ich alles gelernt haben.). You also use it if you have a guess about a connected action in the future (Sie wird vermutlich zu spät in der Schule angekommen sein.).

The future 1 will be formed with the verb + infinitive.

Person	werden+Infinitive
Ich	werde laufen
Du	wirst laufen
er/sie/es	wird laufen
Wir	werden laufen
Ihr	werdet laufen
Sie	werden laufen

Examples of Futur 1:

Morgen werde ich spät nach Hause kommen.

Heute Abend wirst du dein Zimmer aufräumen.

Am Freitag wird er einen Test schreiben.

Wir werden etwas früher aufstehen.

Werdet ihr am Samstag ins Kino gehen?

Sie werden bestimmt wie immer zu spät kommen.

The future 2 will be formed with a form of werden + Participe 2 + auxiliary verb (haben, sein werden).

Person	werden	Participe 2	Auxiliary verb
ich	werde	(den Test)bestanden	haben
du	wirst	(den Test)bestanden	haben
er/sie/es	wird	(den Test)bestanden	haben
Wir	werden	(den Test)bestanden	haben
Ihr	werdet	(den Test)bestanden	haben
Sie	werden	(den Test)bestanden	haben

Examples of futur 2:

Morgen werde ich die Hausaufgaben gemacht haben.

Bis morgen wirst du dein Zimmer aufgeräumt haben.

Er wird am Samstag gekocht haben, wenn ich nach Hause komme.

Wir werden bis heute Abend den Kasten Bier leer getrunken haben.

Ihr werdet bis morgen alles vorbereitet haben.

Sie werden bis morgen das Auto voll getankt haben.

Exercise

1. Write the sentences in future 1 verb form.

a) Ich laufe in den Park. - Ich ____ in den Park _____.

b) Marcus spielt ein Spiel. – Marcus____ ein Spiel_____.

c) Anna liest ein Buch. - Anna ____ein Buch _____.

d) Wir schreiben ein Test. - Wir ____ein Test_____.

e) Ihr redet zu viel. - Ihr ____ zu viel _____.

What is the plusquamperfect?

The plusquamperfect is a tense which expresses the past. However, we use it differently than the perfect and preterite. The plusquamperfect is only used if you have two different actions that have taken place at different times. Then the action which first took place is told in the plusquamperfekt tense.

An example: Als ich nach hause kam, hatte meine Mutter schon gekocht.

First the mother cooked, so the second part of the sentence, "hatte gekocht," was written in the plusquamperfect.

The first part of the sentence, "ich kam nach hause," also happened in the past, but only after the other action.

Plusquamperfect formation

The plusquamperfect is being formed like the perfect with a form of / sein/haben + Partizip II.

Person	sein	Laufen	Person	haben	essen
ich	war	gelaufen	ich	hatte	gegessen
du	warst	gelaufen	du	hattest	gegessen
er/sie/es	war	gelaufen	er/sie/es	hatte	gegessen
wir	waren	gelaufen	Wir	hatten	gegessen
ihr	wart	gelaufen	Ihr	hattet	gegessen
sie	waren	gelaufen	Sie	hatten	gegessen

Plusquamperfekt sein

Person	Plusquamperfekt sein
ich	war gewesen
du	warst gewesen
er/sie/es	war gewesen
wir	waren gewesen
ihr	wart gewesen
sie	waren gewesen

Plusquamperfect example sentences:

Nachdem sie das ganze Wasser ausgetrunken hatte, war ihr schlecht.

Bevor die Woche zu Ende war, hatte ich schon das gesamte Geld ausgegeben.

Sie waren da gewesen, bevor die anderen kamen.

Nachdem er dich abgeholt hatte, ist er nach Hause gefahren.

Nachdem mich mein Bruder besucht hatte, war der Kühlschrank leer.

Anna ist mit ihrem Fahrrad hingefallen. Zuvor hatte sie beim Fahren auf ihr Handy geguckt.

Exercise

1. Add the right form of haben and sein in the plusquamperfect.

a) Ich ____ gewesen.

b) Du ____ gewesen.

c) Er ____ gehabt.

d) Anna und Markus ____ gelaufen.

e) Ihr ____ gesprungen.

f) Lena ____ eingekauft. g) Du ____ im Urlaub gewesen.

h) Er ____ ein Buch gelesen.

i) Wir ____ einen Brief geschrieben.

What are modal verbs?

Modal verbs should be learned because these little words can change the content of your whole sentence. There is a big difference whether someone has to do, wants to do, or can do something. The German modal verbs are müssen, können, wollen, sollen, dürfen, and und mögen. In the following table you will find the English translation of all German modal verbs:

Modal verbs

Modal verb	English	Example
Dürfen	may	Darf ich dein Handy benutzen? / May I use your phone?
Können	can	Ich kann dich verstehen./ I can understand you.
Mögen	like	Ich mag dich. / I like you.
Müssen	must	Sie muss zur Schule gehen./ She must go to school.
Sollen	shall	Du solltest das lieber nicht machen. / You shall not do that.
Woollen	want	Ich will dieses Kleid./I want this dress.

Examples of modal verbs:

Ich kann Morgen nicht kommen.

Du sollst immer etwas zum Frühstück essen.

Wir müssen leider gehen.

Sie wollen nach Deutschland ziehen.

Er mag solche Bücher nicht.

Ihr dürft euch hier umsehen.

Modal verbs in the subjunctive

If you do not yet know what the subjunctive is and how you make it in German, just look at the chapter about the German subjunctive. In the following table you will also find the modal verbs in the preterite. The formation of the subjunctive in the modal verbs is easier if one already knows the form in the preterite.

Indicative	Subjunctive	Preterite
dürfen	dürften	durften
können	könnten	konnten
mögen	möchten	mochten
müssen	müssten	mussten
sollen	sollten	sollten
wollen	wollten	wollten

Examples of modal verbs in subjunctive:

Wir dürften heute den Kuchen essen.

Könntet ihr Geld bringen?

Möchtet ihr etwas essen?

Ich müsste mit ihm sprechen.

Wir sollten zurückgehen.

Wann wolltet ihr denn vorbeikommen?

Exercise

1. Fill the spaces with the correct modal verbs.

a) Ich ____ (können) heute leider nicht kommen.

b) _____ (müssen) du heute noch deine Hausaufgaben machen?

c) Wir ____ (sollen) das Essen heute vorbereiten.

d) Du ____ (müssen) jetzt aufräumen.

e) Wir ____ (mögen) diese Arbeit nicht.

f) Ihr ____ (dürfen) im Wohnzimmer schlafen.

g) Wir ____ (können) auch schon früher gehen.

What are reflexive verbs?

Reflexive verbs always require a corresponding reflexive pronoun. One differentiates the reflexive verbs between the following:

Real reflexive verbs: always need a reflexive pronoun (sich verlaufen)

Semi-reflexive verbs: this is the direction of the verb; sometimes we need the reflexive pronoun, sometimes not (sich ärgern, er ärgert sie)

False reflexive verbs: the verb can be expressed with the same meaning with and without reflexive pronoun (unlike the false ones, because they change the meaning) (sich anziehen / sie zieht das Kleid an)

Conjugation reflexive verbs

Person	Reflexive verb	Reflexive pronouns
ich	Wasche	mich
du	Wäschst	dich
er/sie/es	Wäscht	sich
wir	Waschen	uns
ihr	Wascht	euch
sic	Waschen	sich

Reflexive verbs list

sich waschen

sich anziehen

sich verlaufen

sich ausziehen

sich ärgern

sich auf etw./jmd. verlassen

sich auskennen

sich entschuldigen

sich erinnern

sich konzentrieren

sich schminken

sich setzen

sich wundern

sich ändern

sich beeilen

sich bewerben

sich bücken

sich gewöhnen

sich kämmen

sich treffen

sich umziehen

Exercise

1, Fill in the spaces with the correct form of reflexive verbs and reflexive pronouns.

a) Ich _____ nicht an meinen Urlaub, er ist zu lange her. (sich erinnern)

Mario _____ über die hohe Telefonrechnung. (sich wundern)

Anna _____ in jeder Stadt, auch mit Stadtplan _____. (sich verlaufen)

Du solltest _____, sonst kommst du nicht mehr rein. (sich beeilen)

Sie wollen _____ alle für die gleiche Stelle _____. (sich bewerben)

What is active and passive?

If the acting person is the subject in a sentence, then the sentence is active. Example: Ich wasche mich jeden Tag.

If the acting person is not the subject of the sentence, then the sentence is passive. Example: Das Baby wird jeden Tag gewäscht. "Das Baby" is the subject of the sentence, but not the acting person. The baby does not clean itself; somebody else does it.

Passive formation

In German, there are two different passive forms- the processual passive, as in the sentence "Ich werde geschminkt," and the passive of condition, "Sie ist geschminkt." The two passive forms are formed differently.

The processual passive is made up of a form of werden + participle II.

Processual passive

Time form	Sentence in passive
Present	Ich werde geschminkt
Preterite	Ich wurde geschminkt.
Perfect	Ich bin geschminkt worden.
Plusquamperfekt	Ich war geschminkt worden.
Futur 1	Ich werde geschminkt werden.
Futur 2	Ich werde geschminkt worden sein.

The passive of condition is formed from a form of sein + Partizip II:

Tense	Sentence in passive
Present	Sie ist geschminkt.
Preterite	Sie war geschminkt.
Perfect	Sie ist geschminkt gewesen.
Plusquamperfect	Sie war geschminkt gewesen.
Futur 1	Sie wird geschminkt sein.
Futur 2	Sie wird geschminkt gewesen sein.

Active and passive sentences

Active

Ich esse Kuchen.

Sie lachen immer.

Er backt den Kuchen für alle.

Wir schwimmen den ganzen Tag.

Ihr sitzt den ganzen Tag.

Du hilfst mir nie mit den Hausaufgaben.

Passive

Mir wurde meine Handtasche geklaut.

Der Kuchen ist gebacken.

Wir wurden gefragt, ob wir in Urlaub wollen.

Euer Computer ist kaputt. gegangen

Der Mann wurde verletzt.

Die Katze ist versorgt.

Exercise

1. Add the correct verb forms in the passive. Pay attention to the tense.

a) Die Häuser _____ neu_____. (werden, bauen)

b) Ich _____, ob ich eine Schwester habe_____. (werden, fragen)

c) Der Computer _____ schon lange nicht mehr_____. (werden, benutzen)

d) Das Auto _____ von einem Mann_____. (werden, einparken)

e) Die Post _____ heute noch nicht _____. (werden, bringen)

Participle 1 and 2

In German, there are two different types of participles. If you have already passed through the tenses, you have already encountered participle 2 and participle perfect in the formation of the perfect. The participle 1, on the other hand, is a form of the present.

Participle 1 formation

Infinitive + d

Infinitive	Participle 1
beobachten	beobachtend
Lichen	lachend

Weinen	weinend
Sagen	sagend
Singen	singend
träumen	träumend
Sein	seiend

Examples with the participle 1:

Die Katze beobachtend stolperte ich über einen Stuhl.

Immer noch lachend über dieses Ereigniss, vergaß ich im Supermarkt das zu kaufen, was ich brauchte.

Weinend stand ich bei der Beerdigung meiner Großeltern.

Träumend vergaß ich alles um mich herum.

Participle 2 formation

Regular verbs: ge + verb base + t

Infinitive	Participle 2
fragen	gefragt
planen	geplant
sagen	gesagt

Regular verbs with the ending -ieren

Infinitive	Participle 2
reparieren	repariert
studieren	studiert
manipulieren	manipuliert

Examples with the participle 2:

Ich habe dich gefragt, ob du einen Bruder hast.

Du hast den Urlaub doch geplant.

Er hat gesagt er kommt heute zu mir.

Wir haben das Badezimmer repariert.

Sie haben 3 Jahre lang studiert.

Ich glaube hier wurde etwas manipuliert.

Exercises

1. In this exercise, the infinitive is in the left column and the corresponding participle 1 is in the right column. Add the correct form to each space.

stehen _____

laufen _____

lachen _____

_____ fragend

_____ trinkend

gehen _____

_____ singend

sagen _____

schreiben _____

2. In this exercise, the infinitives of the verbs are in the left column, and the corresponding participle 2 forms are in the right column. Fill in the spaces.

weinen _____

sagen _____

_____ gearbeitet

_____ gelegen

trinken _____

essen _____

springen _____

sein _____

haben _____

_____ geschrieben

Subjunctive 1 and 2

We use the subjunctive forms in German in indirect speech.

Subjunctive 1: The subjunctive 1 is usually used in news or newspaper texts, but you can also use it in normal linguistic language. Example: Sie sagte sie sei nicht mehr interessiert.

Subjunctive 2: With the subjunctive 2, you can express your ideas or wishes, as well as express yourself in a particularly polite manner. Example: Ich wünschte, ich hätte einen Hund. Dann könnte ich den ganzen Tag mit ihm spielen.

Subjunctive 1 formation

Particularly important in the subjunctive 1 is the verb "sein," because this is the only verb conjugated in all persons. For the other forms, we usually only use the 3rd person singular in German.

sein	Subjunctive 1
ich bin	ich sein
du bist	du seist
er/sie/es ist	er/sie/es sei
wir sind	wir seien
ihr seid	ihr seiet
sie sind	sie seien

In the 3rd person singular, we remove the -n before the infinitive of the verb to make a subjunctive from the indicative form.

3. Person Singular Indicative	3. Person Singular Indicative
er hat	er habe
sie schreibt	sie schreibe
sie liest	sie lese
er fragt	er frage
er muss	Er müsse
sie sagt	sie sage
er lacht	er lache

Examples of subjunctive 1:

Er sagt er habe den Hund gefüttert.

Sie sagt sie habe das Zimmer aufgeräumt.

Er sagt er lache wenig.

Sie sagt sie lese die Zeitung.

Er sagt er schreibe die Hausaufgaben.

Subjunctive 2 formation

You can express the subjunctive 2 both in the present and in the past. For this you need two different forms for the formation.

For the subjunctive 2 in the present form, you attach the conjunctival ending to the base of the preterite form, and strong verbs also receive an umlaut when they contain an o, a, or u.

The conjunctive 2 in the past form is formed from the subjunctive form of sein/haben + Partizip 2.

Subjunctive 2 present form

Person	haben	sein	kommen	würde
1.Pers.Sg.	ich hätte	ich wäre	ich käme	ich würde
2.Pers.Sg.	du hättest	du wärst	du kämst	du würdest
3.Pers.Sg.	er/sie/es hätte	er/sie/es wäre	er/sie/es käme	er/sie/es würde
1.Pers.Pl.	wir hätten	wir wären	wir kämen	wir würden
2.Pers.Pl.	ihr hättet	ihr wärt	ihr kämt	ihr würdet
3.Pers.Pl.	sie hätten	sie wären	sie kämen	sie würden

Weak verbs and mixed verbs are often very similar to the indicative form in the preterite, so we often use the würde form. Example: Ich machte – Ich würde machen.

Subjunctive 2 past form

Person	sein	haben	fragen
1. Pers.Sg.	ich wäre gewesen	ich hätte gehabt	ich hätte gefragt
2. Pers.Sg.	du wärst gewesen	du hättest gehabt	du hättest gefragt
3. Pers.Sg.	er/sie/es wäre	er/sie/es hätte	er/sie/es hätte

	gewesen	gehabt	gefragt
1. Pers.Pl.	wir wären gewesen	wir hätten gehabt	wir hätten gefragt
2. Pers.Pl.	ihr wärt gewesen	ihr hättet gehabt	ihr hättet gefragt
3. Pers.Pl.	sie wären gewesen	sie hätten gehabt	sie hätten gefragt

Conjunctive 2 Examples:

Ich wünschte ich wäre so mutig.

Hätte ich dich gesehen, hätte ich dich begrüßt.

Sie würden mich doch nicht sehen.

Wir sagten wir würden vorbeikommen.

Ich würde jetzt Kuchen essen.

Ich wünschte ich hätte einen Hund.

Hätte ich die Lösungen für den Test gehabt, hätte ich eine gute Note bekommen.

Exercise

1. Fill the spaces with the right subjunctive 1 form.

Er sagte:

a) - er _____ (haben) Hunger.

b) - er _____ (sein) gestern sehr spät nach Hause gekommen.

c) - Marcus und Franko _____ (sein) heute schon um 6 da gewesen.

d) -er _____ (kommen) heute.

e) - du _____ (sein) zuhause.

What is an imperative?

The imperative is a form of command that you use when you want someone to do something or not. Since you are directly addressing the person you are requesting, this form is only for the second person singular and plural, the courtesy form, and in some cases, also the first person plural.

Imperative forms

With the imperative, you ask someone to do or not to do something. If you are angry or parents complain with their children, often a rude form of the imperative is used, in which the "please" is omitted.

Imperative Formation

1. Person plural and the courtesy form: the verb in the infinitive + wir / Sie - Example: Machen wir das Fenster auf! Machen Sie das Fenster auf!

2. Person Singular *: In most cases, you only have to take the infinitive and omit the -en. With some verbs, you still have to add an -e if you want to express yourself, not others. - Example: Sag mir bitte wo du gestern gewesen bist! Lerne den deutschen Imperativ!

2. Person Plural: For this imperative form, simply use the normal form for the second person plural and leave the personal pronoun. Example: Geht jetzt bitte ins Auto.

As always, the form of "sein" is special. In the table below, you will see how to make the imperative with this verb.

Person	sein
2.Person Sg(du)	sei!
2.Person Pl(ihr)	seid!
1.Person Pl(wir)	seien!
Polite form	seien!

* - In the second person, there are a few exceptions. The root vowel is not changed in the imperative as in the normal form (example: du lässt - lass!). In addition, we always attach an -e to verbs that end in the normal form with d or t (example: rate!).

Examples with imperative:

Lass mich bitte in Ruhe!

Räum dein Zimmer auf!

Mach bitte bis heute Abend deine Hausaufgaben!

Iss den Teller bitte leer!

Fahr mich bitte ins Krankenhaus!

Sei nicht immer gleich so zickig!

Seid lieb zueinander!

Seien Sie bitte etwas netter zu meinem Sohn!

Trink bitte dein Glas aus!

Seid nicht so gemein zueinander!

Gehen wir nach Hause!

Seien wir lieb und gehen jetzt schlafen!

Frag mich das nicht!

Besuch deinen Bruder mal wieder!

Exercise

1. Fill the spaces with the correct imperative form. Pay attention to the use of uppercase and lowercase letters at the beginning of the sentence.

a) _____ (gehen) wir ersteinmal nach Hause!

b) _____ (sein) wir nett zueinander!

c) _____ (machen) bitte die Tür zu!

d) _____ (abschließen) dein Fahrrad bitte noch!

e) _____ (aufpassen) gut auf euch ____!

f) _____ (lassen) mich in Ruhe!

g) _____ (trinken) Sie nicht so viel Alkohol, das ist sehr schlecht für die Leber!

Chapter 6 – What are adjectives?

In German, adjectives are also called "property words." They describe how something is, or what qualities something has. The beautiful princess, for example, has the property that she is beautiful. We have three different ways to use adjectives- adverbial and predicative, which do not change their ending depending on the gender and number of the noun, and attributive, which adapt their ending to the gender and number of the noun.

Adverbial adjectives: Adjectives that come after the verb (except: sein, bleiben, werden). Example: Dieser Mann fährt gut Auto.

Predicative adjectives: Adjectives that come after the verbs sein, bleiben, werden. Example: Die Frau ist schön.

Attributive adjectives: They stand before a noun and adap their ending to the noun. Example: Die schöne Frau ist eine gute Autofahrerin.

Declination Adjectives

The German adjectives differ in their endings, depending on whether they follow a certain article / undetermined article or no article.

Definite article

Case	Masculine	Feminine	Neuter	Plural
Nominative	der gute Junge	die gute Frau	das gute Auto	die guten Autos
Genitive	des guten Jungens	der guten Frau	des guten Autos	der guten Autos
Dative	dem guten Jungen	der guten Frau	dem guten Auto	den guten Autos

| Accusative | den guten Jungen | die gute Frau | das gute Auto | die guten Autos |

Indefinite article

Case	Masculine	Feminine	Neuter
Nominative	ein guter Junge	eine gute Frau	ein gutes Auto
Genitive	eines guten Jungens	einer guten Frau	eines guten Autos
Dative	einem guten Jungen	einer guten Frau	einem guten Auto
Accusative	einen guten Jungen	eine gute Frau	ein gutes Auto

No article

Case	Masculine	Feminine	Neuter	Plural
Nominative	guter Junge	gute Frau	gutes Auto	gute Autos
Genitive	guten Jungens	guter Frau	guten Autos	guter Autos
Dative	gutem Jungen	guter Frau	gutem Auto	guten Autos
Accusative	guten Jungen	gute Frau	gutes Auto	gute Autos

Adjectives increasing forms

Comparative: the ending -er. Example: Lena ist schooner als Maria.

Superlative: on or certain article + ending -sten. Example: Lena ist am schönsten. Lena ist die schönste.

Exceptions: gut - besser - am besten; viel - mehr - am meisten; groß - größer - am größten; hoch - höher - am höchsten

Exercise

1. Fill in the spaces with the correct form of the adjectives in parentheses.

Frankfurt ist eine sehr _____ (schön) Stadt. Meine _____ (rot) Tasche ist mit heute geklaut worden.

Ist dein Auto _____ (schnell)?

Du hast einen _____ (klein) Hund.

Meine Tochter ist schon richtig _____ (groß) geworden.

Der Stift gehört dem _____ (klein) Mädchen.

What are adverbs?

Adverbs refer to verbs. In contrast, adjectives refer to nouns. In the sentence "Der große Mann läuft schnell," the adjective would be "groß," because this refers to the noun "man," and the word "schnell" would be the adverb, because this refers to the verb "läuft" and not to the noun. In German, we have four different types of adverbs, which will be explained to you in this chapter.

4 different types of adverbs:

Local adverb (adverbs of place): Answers to the questions: Wo? Wohin? Woher? Examples: hier, dort, überall, hinein, weg, heim, hinten, drinnen, fort, links, rechts, oben, unten. Example sentence: Sie stehen drinnen und warten auf dich!

Temporal adverb (adverbs of time): Answers to the questions: Wann? Seit wann? Wie lange? Bis wann? Examples: heute, gestern, morgen, danach, montags, bald, immer, nie, oft, jetzt, gleich, noch, stets. Example sentence: Ich koche jetzt das essen.

Modal adverb (adverbs of kind or way): Answers to the questions: Wie? Wie sehr? Wie viel? Examples: kaum, ein bisschen. sehr, ganz, genauso, genug, anders, äußerst, beinahe, hoffentlich, fast. Example sentence: Hoffentlich finde ich meinen Hund schnell wieder..

Causal adverb (adverbs of reason): Answers to the questions: Wieso? Weshalb? Warum? Examples: Deshalb, darum, daher, folglich, demnach, somit, trotzdem. Example sentence: Darum brauche ich dringend Urlaub.

In addition, there are **relative adverbs**, which initiate a relative theorem (wo, worüber, wofür, womit), and conjunctival adverbs, which link sentences (außerdem, schließlich, deshalb).

Examples with adverbs:

Ich komme bald nach.

Der Test ist sehr gut gelaufen.

Ich habe ihn nach dem Ort gefragt, wo wir uns treffen.

Ich stand die ganze Zeit direkt hinter dir.

Darum glaube ich, dass es besser ist, die Hausaufgaben jetzt zu machen.

Gefällt dir das Kleid? - Ja es gefällt mir sehr.

Er ist heute aus Bremen gekommen.

Sie sind oft alleine zu Hause.

Exercise

1. Choose the correct word to complete the sentence.

a) Ich habe mir heute frei genommen. _____ muss ich nicht zur Arbeit gehen. (Deshalb, Ganz, Sehr, Anders)

b) _____ möchte ich den ganzen Tag auf dem Sofa liegen und mich entspannen. (Ganz, Morgen, Rechts, Hinein)

c) _____ ist die Prüfungsphase vorbei. (Sehr, Äußerst, Darum, Folglich, Bald)

d) Gefällt dir das neue Sofa? - Ja, _____. (darum, sehr, ganz, bald)

e) Wir warten _____ auf euch. (darum, bald, drinnen, ganz)

Chapter 7 – What are prepositions?

Prepositions are relation words. They describe the relationship between nouns / pronouns and other words. It is important that you know the exact meaning of the pronouns to understand the sentence. As with adverbs, we have different types of prepositions- temporal, local, causal, and modal.

German prepositions list

Preposition type	Preposition	English	Example
Local	neben	next to	Das Haus steht neben der Kirche.
	auf	On	Das Essen steht auf dem Tisch.
	unter	under	Der Stift liegt unter dem Tisch.
	hinter	behind	Er wartet hinter der Kirche.
	vor	in front of	Der Hund steht vor dem Haus.
	zwischen	between	Die Katze schläft zwischen den Autos.
	zu	toward	Sie dreht sich zu ihm um.
	in	in	Ich lebe in einem kleinen Haus.

Temporal	am	on (the)	Am 8. Mai hat er Geburtstag
	vor	before	Vor dem Spiel gehen wir etwas essen.
	nach	after	Nach dem Konzert wird gefeiert.
	um	at	Um 8 Uhr treffen wir uns bei Kathi.
	seit	for/since	Seit 3 Jahren versuche ich einen Job zu finden.
	gegen	around	Gegen 9 gibt es Abendessen.
	ab	from	Ab 8 kannst du mit mir rechnen.
	für	for	Für 5 Jahre muss er ins Gefängnis.
	von...bis	from...to	Von 8-12 schläft unsere Tochter immer.
	zwischen	between	Zwischen 9 und 10 kannst du mich erreichen.
Modal	mit	with	Mit meiner besten Freundin habe ich Spaß.
	ohne	without	Ohne Kaffe am Morgen bin ich müde.
	gegen	against	Er kämpft gegen einen Profi.

	auf	in	Er lernt den Satz auf Deutsch.
	aus	made of	Der Pullover ist aus Wolle.
Causal	aufgrund	because of	Aufgrund dessen habe ich nachgefragt.
	trotz	despite	Trotz des Regens habe ich gute Laune.
	dank	due to	Dank der schlechten Note bekomme ich Ärger.
	laut	according to	Laut meinem Nachbarn wird es heute regnen.
	aus	due to	Aus diesem Grund weigere ich mich.
	bezüglich	regarding	Bezüglich dessen möchte ich mit dir sprechen.
	wegen	because of	Wegen dieser Angelegenheit träume ich schlecht.

Exercise

1. Choose the correct preposition for each space below..

a) Das Essen steht _____ dem Tisch. – auf, unter, hinter

b) _____ Meer schwimmen viele Fische. - Auf, Zu, Im

c) Die Stadt ist _____ Wochenende besonders voll. - am, unter, neben

d) _____ der Woche muss ich immer arbeiten. - Am, Auf, Unter

e) Du kannst so _____ 8 mit meinem Anruf rechnen. - gegen, zu, bei

f) Ich habe jeden Montag _____ 5 Tanztraining. - um, bei, seit

g) ie sind jetzt _____ 5 Wochen ein Paar. - für, zwischen, seit

Chapter 8 – Numbers, date and time

In this chapter, you will learn everything about how we use numbers (cardinal numbers, ordinal numbers) and the date and time in German.

Cardinal numbers

Cardinal numbers are the basic numbers. We use them to indicate how much of something is available.

Spelling

1	eins	11	Elf	21	einundzwanzig	31	einunddreißig
2	zwei	12	zwölf	22	zweiundzwanzig	40	vierzig
3	drei	13	Dreizehn	23	dreiundzwanzig	50	fünfzig
4	vier	14	Vierzehn	24	vierundzwanzig	60	sechzig
5	fünf	15	Fünfzehn	25	fünfundzwanzig	70	siebzig
6	sechs	16	Sechzehn	26	sechsundzwanzig	80	achtzig
7	sieben	17	Siebzehn	27	siebenundzwanzig	90	neunzig
8	acht	18	Achtzehn	28	achtundzwanzig	100	einhundert
9	neun	19	Neunzehn	29	neunundzwanzig	1000	eintausend
10	zehn	20	Zwanzig	30	dreißig	1.000.000	eine Million

We say the one unit numbers before the ten unit numbers and connect both parts with the word "und."

Example:

35 - fünfunddreißig

Hundreds and thousands

Hundreds of thousands can be connected with or without "und", with units or tens. Between thousands and hundreds we do not use "und".

Example:

308 - dreihundert(und)acht

At the beginning of the word, we can cut the numbers einhundert/eintausend to hundert/tausend.

Example:

147 – (ein)hundert(und)siebenundvierzig

1147 – (ein)tausendeinhundert(und)siebenundvierzig

Numbers from 10000 are often separated by a dot or a space for better reading.

Example:

57458302

57 458 302

The numbers up to 999,999 are written as one word.

Example:

999.999- neunhundertneunundneunzigtausendneunhundertneunundneunzig

Year figures up to 1999 are given as hundreds. For all years from 2000, however, we use the normal cardinal numbers.

Example:

1999 – neunzehnhundertneunundneunzig

2011 – zweitausend(und)elf

Millions

From the number 2,000,000 we use the plural. Note that Million is always treated as an extra word.

Example:

1.500.000 – eine Million fünfhunderttausend

2.000.000 – zwei Millionen

47.850.203 – siebenundvierzig Millionen achthundertfünfzigtausendzweihundert(und)drei

Ordinal numbers

We use ordinal numbers for the date or if we want to specify a sequence.

In German, we write the ordinal numbers with a dot.

Example: 1. Oktober 2016

1.	erst...	11.	elft...	21.	einundzwanzigst...	31.	einunddreißigst...
2.	zweit...	12.	zwölft...	22.	zweiundzwanzigst...	40.	vierzigst...
3.	dritt...	13.	dreizehnt...	23.	dreiundzwanzigst...	50.	fünfzigst...
4.	viert...	14.	vierzehnt...	24.	vierundzwanzigst...	60.	sechzigst...
5.	fünft...	15.	fünfzehnt...	25.	fünfundzwanzigst...	70.	siebzigst...
6.	sechst...	16.	sechzehnt...	26.	sechsundzwanzigst...	80.	achtzigst...
7.	siebent.../siebt...	17.	siebzehnt...	27.	siebenundzwanzigst...	90.	neunzigst...
8.	acht...	18.	achtzehnt...	28.	achtundzwanzigst...	100.	einhundertst...
9.	neunt...	19.	neunzehnt...	29.	neunundzwanzigst...	1000.	eintausendst...
10.	zehnt...	20.	zwanzigst...	30.	dreißigst...	1.000.000.	Millionst...

Date: We use the ordinal numbers for the date.

Example:

Heute ist der fünfte Juli.

Das Konzert findet am achtzehnten Februar statt.

Order: We can also specify a sequence with the ordinal numbers.

Example:

Deutsch ist ihre zweite Fremdsprache.

Wir wohnen im vierzehnten Stock.

Enumerations: In enumerations, we merely append the suffix ens. This form is not declined.

Example:

Erstens habe ich keine Lust ins Kino zu gehen, zweitens bin ich pleite und drittens gefällt mir der Film nicht.

Title: When it comes to the title of a person, we write the ordinal number as a Roman numeral with a dot. When speaking, we use the specific article before the ordinal number.

Example:

Friedrich I. – Friedrich der Erste

Elizabeth II - Elizabeth die Zweite

Roman numerals

Mark	I	II	III	IV	V	VI	VII	VIII	IX	X
Value	1	2	3	4	5	6	7	8	9	10

Time

There are various ways of expressing the time in German. For official data (programs, timetables, etc.), the time is indicated with 24 hours. In conversation, we often only use the 12-hour variant.

Formal version

In this version, we first say the hour plus the word "Uhr" and then the minutes.

Example:

10:30 → zehn Uhr dreißig

In German, it is typical with this form to use the 24-hour clock. Thus, confusion is ruled out.

Example:

6:00	sechs Uhr
6:05	sechs Uhr fünf
6:15	sechs Uhr fünfzehn
6:20	sechs Uhr zwanzig
6:30	sechs Uhr dreißig
6:40	sechs Uhr vierzig
6:45	sechs Uhr fünfundvierzig
6:50	sechs Uhr fünfzig

German-language version

Colloquial version

In everyday conversation, we prefer the colloquial version, especially for rough time division.

Example:

10:30 → halb elf

With this type of timing, we can only use the 12-hour clock. To avoid misunderstandings, we can indicate the time of the day (morning, afternoon, evening, night).

Example:

18:30 → (in the evening) (abends) halb sieben

What time is it? - Wie spät ist es?

die Stunde – hour

die Minute – minute

die Sekunde – second

Wie spät ist es? – What time is it?

(Es ist) halb drei. – It's half past two. / It's two thirty.

Viertel nach acht. – Quarter past eight.

Viertel vor zwölf. – Quarter to twelve.

(Es ist) 20 vor zehn. – (It's) twenty to ten.

Zehn nach sieben. – Ten past seven.

(Es ist) 13 Uhr 40. – (It is) one-forty p.m.

von 16:50 Uhr bis 17:30 Uhr – between 4:50 p.m. and 5:30 p.m.

Um wie viel Uhr ist die Prüfung? – What time is the exam / test?

Die Prüfung ist um 15 Uhr. – The exam / test is at 3:00 p.m.

Die Prüfung dauert 60 Minuten. – The exam / test takes 60 minutes.

Date

For the date, we speak and write the day as an ordinal number. For the month, we can either use the ordinal number or the month name. In the spoken language and the addition by the weekday, we usually prefer the month name.

Example:

05/10/2016

5. Oktober 2016

Dienstag, 5. Oktober 2016

Pronunciation of numbers by day (and month)

When writing or speaking, the ordinal numbers receive corresponding adjectives. The month as a number will be added.

1.	erst...	11.	elft...	21.	einundzwanzigst...
2.	zweit...	12.	zwölft...	22.	zweiundzwanzigst...
3.	dritt...	13.	dreizehnt...	23.	dreiundzwanzigst...
4.	viert...	14.	vierzehnt...	24.	vierundzwanzigst...
5.	fünft...	15.	fünfzehnt...	25.	fünfundzwanzigst...
6.	sechst...	16.	sechzehnt...	26.	sechsundzwanzigst...
7.	siebent.../siebt...	17.	siebzehnt...	27.	siebenundzwanzigst...
8.	acht...	18.	achtzehnt...	28.	achtundzwanzigst...
9.	neunt...	19.	neunzehnt...	29.	neunundzwanzigst...
10.	zehnt...	20.	zwanzigst...	30.	dreißigst...
31.	einunddreißigst...				

Months

1.	Januar	(Jan)	7.	Juli	(Jul)
2.	Februar	(Feb)	8.	August	(Aug)
3.	März	(Mär)	9.	September	(Sep)
4.	April	(Apr)	10.	Oktober	(Okt)
5.	Mai	(Mai)	11.	November	(Nov)
6.	Juni	(Jun)	12.	Dezember	(Dez)

Pronunciation of the year figures

From the year 1100 until the year 1999, the years are called hundreds. Starting from the year 2000, we use the normal cardinal numbers.

Chapter 9 - German on the road

In this chapter, you will get the opportunity to learn the basic and most common words used when traveling by train, plane, or car and when staying in a hotel, eating in a restaurant, and similar occasions.

The journey by train

der Zug – the train

die Zugfahrt - the train ride

die Zugverbindung / die Verbindung - the connection / link

die Reservierung - the reservation

den Zug verpassen - miss the train

die Abfahrt - departure

planmäßig - as scheduled

planmäßige - departure as scheduled

die Ankunft – the arrival

ankommen – to arrive

der Bahnhof - the station

der Hauptbahnhof – the main station

der Bahnsteig – the platform

das Gleis – the track

die Hinfahrt – outward journey

die Rückfahrt – homeward journey

eine einfache Fahrt – one-way trip

eine Rückfahrkarte (hin und zurück) – return ticket

erster Klasse – first class

zweiter Klasse – second class

einsteigen – to get on

aussteigen – to get out

umsteigen – to change (trains)

verkehren – to run

durchfahren – go through

fahren über – drive above

dauern - to take a length of time

der Werktag – workday

werktags – on workdays

täglich - daily

das Wochenende - the weekend

With the car to the airport

die Auskunft - information

der Flughafen - airport

die Ampel – traffic lights

der Fußgänger - pedestrian

der Autofahrer – car driver

etwas erklären – to explain something

etwas erkennen – to recognize something

umdenken – to think over

warten – to wait

vorschreiben – to prescribe

fahren – to drive

abbiegen - to turn

rechts - right

links - left

vorne - front

hinten - back

geradeaus – straight ahead

die Straße – the street

der Ring – ring road

breit - wide

vierspurig – four-laned

das Schild - sign

ausgeschildert sein – to be sign posted

etwas verfehlen – to miss something

Travel by plane

das Flugzeug / die Maschine – the aircraft/the machine

der Flug – the flight

fliegen – to fly

der Start – the start

starten – to start

die Landung – the landing

landen – to land

der Abflug – the flight (departure)

abfliegen – to depart

die Ankunft – the arrival

ankommen – to arrive

die Bordkarte – the boarding ticket

der Ausgang – the exit

der Eingang – the entrance

einchecken – the check in

der Ausweis – ID

der Pass – pass

der Reisepass – passport

Raucher - smoker

Nichtraucher – non-smoker

der Gang – aisle

das Fenster - window

der Fensterplatz – seat by window

die Mitte – the middle

die Platzangst - claustrophobia

die Waage - scale

wiegen – to weigh out

das Gepäck – luggage

der Koffer – suitcase

die Reisetasche – travelling bag

der Laptop T- laptop

das Handgepäck – hand luggage

The gas station

der Preis – the price

der Benzinpreis – price of petrol/fuel/gas

hoch - high

hohe Preise – high prices

niedrig - low

niedrige Preise – low prices

der Tank – fuel tank

voll - full

leer - empty

die Tankstelle – the gas station

der Kiosk – kiosk

tanken – to tank up, to get gas

die Zapfsäule – petrol/ gas pump

der Sprit – fuel/gas

das Benzin - petrol

Normal - normal

Super - super

bleifreies Super - super unleaded

Diesel - diesel

Bleifrei - unleaded

verbleit - leaded

putzen – to clean

die Scheibe - windscreen

der Wassereimer - water bucket

kontrollieren – to control

prüfen – to check

der Reifendruck - tire pressure

das Öl – the oil

der Ölstand - oil level

beinahe – almost/nearly

nirgendwo - nowhere

überall – everywhere

Hotel

die Übernachtung – overnight stay

das Bad = das Badezimmer – bath, bathroom

das WC = die Toilette - water closet, toilet

die Dusche – the shower

die Badewanne – the bath, tub

inklusive - inclusive

das Frühstück - breakfast

der Garten - garden

die Vollpension – full board

die Halbpension – half board

der Wochentag – week day

Montag, Dienstag, Mittwoch, Donnerstag, Freitag, Samstag, Sonntag – Monday, Tuesday, Wednesday, Thursday, Friday, Saturday, Sunday

diesen Montag – this monday

nächsten Dienstag – next tuesday

kommenden Mittwoch – the coming wednesday

die Woche – the week

diese Woche – this week

die nächste Woche – next week

die kommende Woche – coming week

nachschauen = nachsehen - check

der Moment – the moment

bleiben – to stay

etwas frei haben – having something free

etwas festmachen – arrange something

der Name – the name

buchstabieren – to spell

einen Namen buchstabieren – to spell a name

The front desk

der Name – name

das Zimmer - room

der Augenblick = der Moment - moment

der Kollege / die Kollegin – the colleague

der Tag - day

die Nacht - night

der Nachtdienst – night duty

der Schlüssel - key

das Zimmer - room

der Stock / das Stockwerk - floor

der Aufzug / der Lift - elevator

richtig - correct

falsch - wrong

links - left

rechts - right

heute - today

morgen - tomorrow

gestern - yesterday

reservieren - reserve

servieren – to serve

wecken – to wake up

die Rechnung – the bill

der Übernachtungspreis - price per night, the price for staying overnight

die Kosten (Pl.) – the prices

das Bargeld - cash

zahlen – to pay

bar zahlen – pay with cash

mit Scheck zahlen - to pay by cheque

mit Kreditkarte zahlen – to pay with credit card

das Telefonat – the phone call

das Getränk – drink

die Minibar – mini bar

gefallen – to like

sich beklagen – to make a complaint

etwas vergessen – to forget something

selbstverständlich – certainly / but of cours

Restaurant

der Tisch – the table

die Person (Pl.: die Personen) – person

ein Tisch für vier Personen – a table for four people

reservieren – to reserve

freihalten – to keep free

der Abend – the evening

abends – in the evening

morgen Abend – tomorrow night

die Uhrzeit – the time

zwischen (temporal) - between

zwischen sieben und acht Uhr – between seven and eight o'clock

die Ecke – corner

das Fenster – window

das Problem – problem

Restaurant arrival

jemandem folgen – follow someone

in der Ecke – in the corner

am Fenster – by the window

auf der Terrasse – on the terrace

hinten / vorne - behind, at the back / at the front

dort drüben – right there

dort hinten – right behind

neben (+ Dativ) – beside, next to

sich etwas wünschen – wish something

etwas mitnehmen – take something

gemütlich - comfortable

die Garderobe – the wardrobe

die Treppe - stairs

die Jacke - jacket

etwas hängen – hang something

die Karte, die Speisekarte – food menu

die Getränkekarte – drink menu

etwas bestellen – order something

die Bestellung – the order

das Mineralwasser, der Sprudel – mineral water

die Kohlensäure – fizz

Mineralwasser mit Kohlensäure - sparkling mineral water, mineral water with gas

Mineralwasser ohne Kohlensäure - sparkling mineral water, mineral water without gas

jemandem etwas bringen – bring something to someone

die Auswahl - selection

eine reiche Auswahl – large range/selection

sich entscheiden – to decide

die Entscheidung - decision

eine Entscheidung treffen – make a decision

jemandem etwas empfehlen – recommend something to someone

Recht haben – to be right

jeden Tag = every day

ganz frisch – really fresh

direkt vom Feld – directly from the field

etwas anderes – something else

die Abwechslung – a change

die Vorspeise - starter

die Hauptspeise – main course

die Nachspeise, das Dessert - dessert

der Salat - salad

der gemischte Salat – mixed salad

die Beilage – side dish

Nudeln, Reis, Kartoffeln, Gemüse – pasta, rice, potato, vegetables

der Lammrücken - roast of lamb, roast saddle of lamb

der Rotwein – red wine

der Beaujolais - Beaujolais

der Weißwein – white wine

kräftig - strong

fruchtig - fruity

wunderbar – wonderful

Ordering dessert

der Nachtisch - dessert

das Dessert - dessert

die Dessertkarte – dessert menu

die Erdbeere - strawberry

die Sahne - cream

das Vanilleeis - vanilla ice-cream

der Espresso – espresso

Introducing yourself and making plans

sich vorstellen – to introduce oneself

der Name – name

der Vorname – first name, given name

der Nachname – last name, surname, e.g. Kaminski, Neumann, Yilmaz, Bauer

Wie ist Ihr Name? (formell) – What is your name? (formal)

Mein Name ist Philipp Neumann. – My name is Philipp Neumann.

Wie heißt du? (informell) – What's your name? (informal)

Ich heiße Franziska. – My name is Franziska.

Wie alt bist du? – How old are you?

Ich bin 20 Jahre alt. – I am 20 years old.

arbeiten – to work, to work full-time

studieren – to study at a university

eine Ausbildung machen – to do an apprenticeship

To greet/ to say goodbye

sich begrüßen – to greet (each other)

Guten Morgen! – Good morning!

Guten Tag, Frau Steller! (formell) – Hello, Ms. Steller! (formal)

Guten Abend, Herr Richter! (formell) – Good evening, Mr. Richter! (formal)

Hallo! (informell) – Hi!/ Hello! (informal)

sich verabschieden – to say goodbye

Auf Wiedersehen! (formell) – Goodbye! (informal)

Tschüss! (informell) – Bye! (informal)

Schönen Tag noch. – Have a good day!

Gute Nacht. – Good night.

Schlaf gut! – Sleep well!

Ask for help

Entschuldigung. – Sorry.

Können Sie mir helfen? – Can you help me?

Ich habe eine Frage. – I have a question.

Ich spreche nicht gut Deutsch. – I do not speak German well.

Ich verstehe das nicht. – I don't understand that.

Was heißt das? – What does that mean?

Wie bitte? – I beg your pardon?

Sprechen Sie bitte langsam. – Please speak slowly.

Wie heißt das auf Deutsch? – What does that mean in German?

Können Sie das bitte wiederholen? – Could you please repeat that?

Vielen Dank! – Thank you very much!

How are you?

Wie geht es Ihnen? (formell) – How are you? (formal)

Sehr gut. – Very well.

Wie geht es dir? (informell) – How are you? (informal)

Mir geht es super. – I'm doing very well.

Mir geht es gut. – I'm fine.

Mir geht es nicht so gut. – Not so well. / I'm not so well.

Mir geht es schlecht. – I'm not doing well. / I feel bad.

Mir geht es beschissen. (umgangssprachlich) – I feel crappy. (colloquial)

Ich bin müde. – I'm tired.

Ich bin krank. – I'm sick.

Ich bin erkältet. – I have a cold.

Ich bin gestresst. – I'm stressed out.

What is your phone number?

0 (null) – 0 (zero)

1 (eins) – 1 (one)

2 (zwei) – 2 (two)

3 (drei) – 3 (three)

4 (vier) – 4 (four)

5 (fünf) – 5 (five)

6 (sechs) – 6 (six)

7 (sieben) – 7 (seven)

8 (acht) – 8 (eight)

9 (neun) – 9 (nine)

10 (zehn) – 10 (ten)

Wie ist deine Telefonnummer? – What's your phone number?

Wie ist deine E-Mail-Adresse? – What's your email address?

der Anruf - the call

das Telefonat = das Telefongespräch - phone call

die Sorge - concern

Bescheid geben / sagen (+Dativ) - to inform, to let someone know

die Verabredung - appointment

das Treffen - meeting

der Treffpunkt - meeting point

klappen = funktionieren – to work out

etwas mit jdm. Ausmachen

= sich mit jdm. verabreden - to make an appointment with someone,

To arrange to meet someone

sich treffen - meet up

sich um 10 Uhr treffen - meet up at 10 o' clock

von Samstag bis Montag – from Saturday to Monday

gleich am Montag = direkt am Montag – this Monday already

vielleicht = eventuell = möglicherweise - maybe, eventually, possibly

Zeit haben - having time

etwas vorhaben = etwas geplant haben – to have plans

sich freuen (auf + Akkusativ) - to be happy about something, to look forward to something

toll = prima - great

die Stimme - voice

die Erkältung - the cold

der Schnupfen – the cold

die Grippe - flu

das Fieber - fever

der Husten - cough

die Sommergrippe - summer flu

verschnupft sein - to have a cold, to have a blocked up nose

erkältet sein - to have a cold, to be sick with a cold

eine Erkältung haben - to have a cold

Schnupfen haben - to to have the sniffles, to have a runny/blocked up nose

der Termin - appointment

die Verabredung - appointment

eine Verabredung haben - to have an appointment

sich verabreden (mit + Dativ) - to make an appointment

jemanden kennen lernen – get to know someone/meet someone

jemanden persönlich kennen lernen - get to know someone personally

jemanden dabei haben - having someone with you

hoffen - hope

stören - disturb

selbstverständlich = natürlich - of course

schlimm, schlimmer, am schlimmsten - bad, worse, the worst

von allen Seiten – from all sides

der Name - the name

der Praktikant, die Praktikantin - trainee/intern (male, female)

Mädchen für alles - dogsbody

das Büro - office

die Besprechung - meeting

das Gespräch - conversation

die Dauer - duration

glauben - believe

kennen (+Akkusativ) - to know

heißen - to be called

finden (+Akkusativ) – to find

suchen (+Akkusativ) - to search

dauern - to last, to take (a length of time)

lange dauern - to last long

wiederkommen = zurück kommen - come again, come back

gleich nebenan = direkt nebenan – right next door

etwa = ungefähr - approximately

vorankommen - to make progress

ein gutes Stück vorankommen - to make considerable progress

zufrieden sein - be satisfied

der Verlauf = die Entwicklung - the progress

mit dem Verlauf zufrieden sein - being satisfied with the progress

sich etwas aufbewahren - to keep something for later

jemandem etwas überlassen - to leave something to someone

jemandem eine Entscheidung überlassen - to make someone other make the decision

die freie Wahl haben – having a free choice

eine Wahl treffen - making a decision

eine gute Idee - a good idea

eine glänzende Idee (= eine sehr gute Idee) - a great idea

jemanden einladen - to invite someone

jemanden abholen - to pick someone up

im Grunde (= eigentlich) - really, basically

recht sein (+ Dativ) - to be right

lieber sein (+ Dativ) - to prefer

das Telefonat - the phone call

etwas erledigen - to get something done, to take care of something

At the post office and at the bank

die Post - post office

die Passage - arcade

die Öffnungszeiten - opening-times

die Mittagspause - lunch-break

der Ruhetag - closed for the day, closing day

über Mittag geöffnet haben - to be open over lunch

über Mittag geschlossen haben / sein - to be closed over lunch

von 8 Uhr bis 18 Uhr durchgehend geöffnet haben / sein - to be open from 8 am through till 6 pm

sich befinden - to be at

geradeaus gehen - go ahead

rechts abbiegen - to turn right

nach links abbiegen - to turn left

auf der linken Seite - on the left side

gegenüber - on the other side, opposite

neben (+ Dat.) - next to, beside

nach 100 Metern nach links abbiegen - turn left after 100 meters

nach 100 Metern rechts einbiegen - turn right after 100 meters

die erste (zweite, dritte, vierte …) Straße links - the first(second, third, fourth...) street to the left

eine Straße überqueren – pass the street

die Bank – the bank

die Wechselstube - currency exchange office

der Schalter - counter

der Geldschalter - money counter

der Bankschalter - bank counter

der Geldautomat - cashpoint, ATM

die Kreditkarte - credit card

die EC-Karte - EC card

die Scheckkarte - cheque card

Geld von seinem Konto abheben - to withdraw money from one's account

Geld wechseln = Geld umtauschen - to exchange money

die Währung - currency

mit Kredit- oder EC-Karte bezahlen – pay with credit or EC card

bargeldlos bezahlen - to pay with plastic

die Öffnungszeiten - the opening hours

verlängerte Öffnungszeiten - longer opening hours

um 17 Uhr schließen - close at 17 o'clock

in der Nähe - nearby

in der näheren Umgebung - in the near vicinity, nearby

in der Gegend - in the area

in der Innenstadt - in the city centre

außerhalb - outside

zu Fuß - by foot

mit der S-Bahn - with the tram

mit der U-Bahn - with the underground

fünf Minuten entfernt sein – being 5 minutes away

das Britische Pfund - pound

der Euro - euro

der Wechselkurs - exchange rate

der Betrag - amount

die Gebühr - fee

Geld wechseln = Geld umtauschen - exchange money

Pfund in Euro wechseln - exchange pound to euro

eine Gebühr verlangen = eine Gebühr berechnen - to ask for a fee

das Centstück - a one-cent coin

das Zweicentstück - a two-cent coin

das Fünfcentstück - a five-cent coin

das Zweieurostück - two-euro coin

der Fünfeuroschein = der Fünfer - a five-euro bill; a fiver

der Zehneuroschein = der Zehner - a ten-euro bill; a tenner

der Zwanzigeuroschein = der Zwanziger - a twenty-euro bill

der Fünfzigeuroschein = der Fünfziger - a fifty-euro bill

der Hunderteuroschein = der Hunderter - a hundred-euro bill

Chapter 10 – Most common words

List of the 500 most common words in German language

A

ab – from, away

der Abend – the evening

der Affe – the ape

alle - all

allein - alone

als – as, than (in comparisons)

also - so

alt - old

an - at

andere – other

der Anfang – the beginning

die Angst – the fear

ankommen – to arrive

die Antwort – the answer

antworten – to answer

anziehen – to dress, to wear

der Apfel – the apple

die Arbeit – the work

arbeiten – to work

der Arm – the arm

der Arzt – the doctor

auch - also

auf - on

die Aufgabe – the task, the exercise

das Auge, die Augen – the eye, the eyes

aus – out of, from

das Auto – the car

B

der Bär – the bear

baden – to bathe

bald - soon

der Ball – the ball

bauen – to build

der Baum – the tree

der Bauer – the farmer

beginnen – to begin

bei – at

beide – both

das Bein – the leg

das Beispiel – the example

bekommen – to get

der Berg – the mountain

das Bett – the bed

bezahlen – to pay

das Bild – the picture

bin – (I) am
bist – (you) are
blau - blue
bleiben – to remain
die Blume – the flower
der Boden – the floor
böse - evil
brauchen – to need
braun - brown
der Brief – the letter
bringen – to bring
das Brot – the bread
der Bruder – the brother
das Buch – the book

D

da – there
dachte – (I, he, she, it) thought
dann – then
denken – to think
deshalb – because of that
diese - these
das Ding – the thing
das Dorf – the village
dick – thick, fat
doch – but
draussen – outside
drehen - turn

drei - three

dumm - stupid

durch – through

dürfen – to be allowed

durfte – (I, he, she, it) was allowed to do

dabei – with it, at that

damit – with this

daran – about that

davon – of that

E

die Ecke – the corner

das Ei – the egg

ein - a

einfach – simple

einige - some

das Eis – the ice, the ice cream

der Elefant – the elephant

die Eltern – the parents

das Ende – the end

endlich - finally

er - he

die Erde – the Earth

erklären – to explain

erschrecken – to scare

erst - first

erzählen – to tell, to narrate

es - it

essen – to eat

das Essen – the food

etwas – something

F

fährt – (he, she, it) drives

fahren – to drive

das Fahrrad – the bicycle

fallen – to fall

die Familie – the family

fangen – to catch

fast – nearly

fehlen – to miss

der Fehler – the mistake

das Fenster – the window

die Ferien – the holidays

fertig - ready

fest – fixed, steady

fiel – (I, he, she, it) fell

finden – to find

der Finger – the finger

der Fisch – the fish

die Flasche – the bottle

fliegen- to fly

die Frage – the question

fragen – to ask

die Frau – the woman

frei - free

der Freund – the friend

fressen – to eat (for animals)

die Freude – the joy

freuen – to be happy

der Freund – the friend

früh – early

fünf - five

für – for

fuhr – (I, he, she, it) drove

der Fuß – the foot

der Fußball – the football

G

gab – (I, he, she, it) gave

ganz – totally

der Garten – the garden

geben – to give

gebissen – bit

der Geburtstag – the birthday

gegen – at about

gehen – to walk

gehören – to belong

gelb - yellow

das Geld – the money

genau – exactly

gerade – straight, just about

gern – with pleasure

die Geschichte – the stort, history

geschrieben – written

das Gesicht – the face

gestellt – placed

gesund – healthy

gibt – (he, she, it) gives

ging – (I, he, she, it) went

das Glas – the glass

glauben – to believe

gleich – soon

das Glück – the happiness

glücklich - happy

groß – great, big

grün - green

gut – good

H

das Haar, die Haare – the hair, hairs

haben – to have

hängen – to hang

halb - half

der Hals – the neck

halten – to hold

die Hand – the hand

der Hase – the hare

hast – (you) have

hat – (he, she, it) has

hatte – (I, he, she, it) had

das Haus – the house

heiss – hot

heißen – to be called

heißt – (he, she, it) is called (i.e. My/his name is...)

heizen – to heat

helfen – to help

heraus – out of

Herr – Mr.

heute – today

hier - here

der Himmel – the heaven, sky

hinein – into

hinter - behind

hoch - high

hören – to hear

holen – to bring over

die Hose – the trousers

der Hund – the dog

der Hunger – the hunger

der Hut – the hat

I

ich - I

der Igel – the hedgehog

im - in

immer - always

in - in

ist – (he, she, it) is

J

ja - yes

das Jahr, die Jahre – the year, the years

jeder - each

jetzt - now

jung - young

der Junge – the boy

K

kälter – colder

der Kaffee – the coffee

kalt – cold

kam – (I, he, she, it) came

kann – can

kaputt - broke

die Katze – the cat

kaufen – to buy

kein – no

keiner – no one

kennen – to know

das Kind – the child

die Klasse – the class

klein – small

kochen – to cook

der König – the king

können – can

könnte - could

kommen – to come

der Kopf – the head

kräftig - strong

krank – sick

die Küche – the kitchen

die Kuh – the cow

kurz – short

der Kuss – the kiss

L

lachen – to laugh

lag – (I, he, she, it) lay

das Land – the country

lang – long

langsam - slow

las – (I, he, she, it) read

lassen – to let

laufen – to run

laut – loud

leben – to live

der Lehrer, die Lehrerin – the teacher

leer – empty

leicht – easy, light

leise - quiet

legen – to lie (s.th down)

lernen – to learn

lesen – to read

letzte – the last

Leute - people

das Licht – the light

lieb – dear

lief – (I, he, she, it) ran

liegen – to lie (down)

ließ – (I, he, she it) let

das Loch – the hole

der Löwe – the lion

los – loose, off

die Luft – the air

lustig – funny

M

machen – to make

das Mädchen – the girl

mal – times (as in: three times)

malen – to paint

man – one (as in: one should do this)

der Mann – the man

die Maus – the mouse

mehr - more

mein, meinen – my

Menschen – people

merken – to notice

die Milch – the milk

die Minute – the minute

mit – with

mögen – to like

müssen, muss – must

die Mutter, Mutti – the mother

N

nach – after, to (a city, country)

nachher – afterwards

nächste – next

die Nacht – the night

nämlich – namely

nah – close

nahm – (I, he, she it) took

der Name, die Namen – the name, the names

die Nase – the nose

nass - wet

natürlich – naturally

neben – next to, beside

nehmen – to take

nennen – to name

nein - no

neu – new

nicht – not

nichts – nothing

nie – never

nimmt – (he, she, it) takes

noch – still, another

nun – now

nur – only

O

oben – on top, above

ob – whether

oben – above

offen – open

oft – often

ohne – without

das Ohr, die Ohren – the ear, the ears

die Oma – the grandmother (also: die Grossmutter)

der Onkel – the uncle

P

packen – to pack

das Pferd – the horse

pflanzen – to plant

die Pfütze – the puddle

der Platz – the place, the square

plötzlich – suddenly

R

das Rad – the wheel

rechnen – to calculate

reich – rich

reiten – to ride

rennen – to run

richtig – correct

rief – (I, he, she, it) called

rot – red

rufen – to call

ruhig – quiet

rund – round

S

die Sache – the thing

sagen – to say

sah – (I, he, she, it) saw

satt – full, well fed

schenken – to give (as a present)

schicken – to send

das Schiff – the ship

schimpfen – to rant

schlafen - to sleep

schlagen – to hit

schlecht, schlimm – bad

der Schnee – the snow

schnell - quick

schon - already

schön - beautiful

schon - already

schreiben – to write

schreien – to scream

der Schüler – the pupil

der Schuh – the shoe

die Schule – the school

schwarz – black

schwer – difficult, heavy

die Schwester – the sister

schwimmen – to swim

der See – the lake

die See – the sea

sehen – to see

sehr – very

sein – to be

die Seite – the side

selbst - even

setzen – to sit

sieben - seven

sind – (we, they) are

singen – to sing

sitzen – to sit

so – so

sofort – suddenly

der Sohn – the son

soll – should, shall

der Sommer – the summer

die Sonne – the sun

der Sonntag – the Sunday

spät – late

der Spaß – the fun

das Spiel – the game

spielen – to play

sprechen – to talk

springen – to jump

die Stadt – the city, the town

stand – (I, he, she, it) stood

stark - strong

stehen – to stand

steigen – to climb

der Stein – the stone

stellen – to place

die Straße – the street

das Stück – the piece

der Stuhl – the chair

die Stunde – the hour

suchen – to search

T

der Tag – the day

tanken – to refuel

die Tante – the aunt

die Tasse – the cup

der Teller – the plate

tief - deep

das Tier – the animal

der Tisch – the table

die Tochter – the daughter

tot - dead

tragen – to carry

traurig – sad

treffen – to meet

trinken – to drink

tun – to do
die Tür – the door

U
über – above, about
die Uhr – the clock
um - at
und - and
unten – below
unter – under

V
der Vater, Vati – the father
vergessen – to forget
verkaufen – to sell
verlieren – to lose
verstecken – to hide
viel – many
viele – a lot of
vielleicht – perhaps
vier - four
der Vogel – the bird
voll – full
vom, von - of
vor – before
vorbei – past (a building)

W

der Wagen – the car, the carriage

wahr - true

der Wald – the forest

war – was

warm - warm

warten – to wait

warum - why

was – what

waschen - to wash

das Wasser – the water

der Weg – the way

weg – away

Weihnachten – Christmas

weil – because

weinen – to cry

weiß - white

weit, weiter – far, futher

wenig – few

wenn – when, if

wer – who

werfen – to throw

wie – how

wieder – again

die Wiese – the meadow

wild – wild

der Winter – the winter

wir – we

wissen - to know

wo – where

die Woche – the week

wohnen – to live

wollen (ich will, du willst...) – want (I want, you want...)

das Wort – the word

die Wurst – the sausage

Z

die Zahl – the number

der Zahn – the tooth

zehn – ten

zeigen – to show

die Zeit – the time

die Zeitung – the newspaper

ziehen – to draw

das Zimmer – the room

zu – to (e.g. die Zeit zu gehen = the time to leave)

zuerst – first of all

der Zug – the train

zurück – back

zusammen – together

zwei - two

Conclusion

A second language is a first-class investment. You can learn new social skills , learn about different lifestyles and cultures, and even meet new friends in other countries. When you decide to learn a language and really dedicate yourself to practicing, you will always open new doors with much better chances for the future. But most importantly, you will experience it as a personal success.

There are many reasons why it is useful to learn the German language. You will be able to find a very demanding job, for example. One becomes more indispensable in a company and increases the chance for promotion possibilities. Many international companies are based in Germany and attach great importance to the multilingualism of their employees. For a secure, professional career, the learning of the German language is almost indispensable. In addition, there are also many other benefits, as German also plays a major role in science and technology, literature, art, and philosophy.

You see there are many reasons to learn German. You just have to practice and use this book to improve your skills.

If you are still not convinced about learning German, just remember what Goethe once said:

"Wer fremde Sprachen nicht spricht, weiß nichts von seiner eigenen"

"Those who do not speak foreign languages, know nothing about their own."

Part 2: German Short Stories

9 Simple and Captivating Stories for Effective German Learning for Beginners

Introduction

How do you learn to write well? How do you expand your vocabulary? How can you improve your ability to express your thoughts and ideas? How can you improve your foreign language skills in a pleasant and varied way? A reasonable way is undoubtedly: to read as much as possible! For this reason, we warmly recommend that you read the stories in this book if you want to learn more words and improve your verbal or written expression. We made it easy for you to read these interesting stories by simply offering a translation in English. You can learn some new words and answer questions about them at the end. This is a way to learn German and still have fun.

Through regular reading you get a feeling for the foreign language and for the sentence structure and you can see how vocabulary is used in the context and get to know lots of new words. Do not be confused by unknown structures. Just read - you do not read to study grammar, but to read with pleasure, right? In the beginning, it is certainly better to try to understand the story in German, but if you need some help, you have everything you need in English. So start with small steps and work your way through slowly. But the most important step is: just start and read regularly, preferably every day.

The advantages of reading are obvious. Reading broadens the human horizon, enriching its inner world, making it more intelligent, and positively impacting memory. It is also important to read because reading expands the vocabulary and promotes the development of clearer thinking, which allows one to clearly formulate and express thoughts. It will definitely help you to express yourself and choose the right words. This is why you should take a look at the stories we have for you. Try to read them and just have fun!

Chapter 1 – How to read effectively

Effective reading is not about being as fast as possible, but about understanding the content and keeping it in mind. To understand when effective reading is especially helpful, two different ways of reading must be distinguished:

Pleasure. Of course, when you're reading for yourself, effectiveness is not the first thing you think about. Nevertheless, it can increase your reading pleasure. Effective reading can help you appreciate your book even more through better understanding.

Learning. Anyone who has ever had to read several books for an exam knows how valuable and helpful effective reading can be. It saves time, energy, and in the case of learning, it can make everything easier.

When reading the stories, enjoyment and a sense of achievement are vitally important because that keeps you coming back for more. The more you read, the more you learn. The best way to enjoy reading and to feel that sense of achievement is by reading entire chapters from beginning to end. Consequently, reaching the end of a book is the most important thing ... more important than understanding every word in it! And this brings us to the single most important point: You don't need to understand everything you read. This is completely normal and to be expected. The fact that you do not know a word or phrase does not mean that you're "stupid" or "not good enough." It simply means you're engaged in the language learning process, just like everybody else.

So what should you do when there's something you do not understand? Sooner or later you can get to a point where you don't understand something. A foreign word, a concept or a phrase - nobody knows everything. Therefore, take the time to look up these things to really understand it. The same applies if, for example, in context people or places are mentioned which you can not assign to something. The more accurate your information, the better you will understand the content. If you find yourself stumped by an unknown word, here are five ways to tackle the problem:

Look at the word and see if it's familiar in any way. Take a guess - you might surprise yourself! Go back and read the word a few times. Using the context of that sentence, and everything else that's happening in the story, try to guess what the unknown word might mean. This takes practice, but is often easier than you think! If you can't find the word in the translation or in the vocabulary list, write the word down and find the meaning later. Then keep reading.

Sometimes, you might find a word that is in the past tense or that looks unfamiliar. For example:

Wohnte (inf. Wohnen) – lived (live)

Nahm (inf. nehmen) – took (take)

Kam (inf. Kommen) – came (come)

You may not recognize the word at first, but you can look at the whole sentence and see if something would make sense. You may get it on your own. Don't be frustrated.

Stages of learning to read a text:

Learn to recognize individual words and phrases.

Try to understand the meaning of the sentence by looking at the translation.

Learn to read simple sentences, looking up words when necessary.

Learn to understand a complex text with occasional reference to a dictionary.

The key factors to your success are:

A passionate obsession for your target language and the work you want to read.

A love for learning (languages).

An understanding of how to learn, including language methods and progress tracking.

Most language learners can't enjoy reading because they think of every single word, "Why does the word have this ending?", "Why is this time used?", "Why are these subjunctive forms used all the time?", "Why is this word now actually behind this and not before? ". Free yourself from wanting to analyze everything. If you're reading, it's all about understanding the text. If you want to do grammatical analysis, you have other materials at your disposal. Your brain can not concentrate on ten thought processes at the same time. You are so "killing" the fun.

One of the best ways to approach reading correctly is the "double reading method." With this method, you read the story completely, without thinking whether you have understood the text now or not. Then you try to summarize the text. Try to fix your brain on the most important points that caused the most emotions in the chapter. Then you read the chapter again and realize that it has become easier to understand the full text. This time, you can also focus more on the details and be more emotionally connected to the characters in the story.

With time, you'll see that you understand each story better. Don't force yourself and don't give up. We hope that you'll enjoy these wonderful stories below!

Chapter 2 – Der Mann und das Pferd (The man and the horse)

Es war einmal ein armer Mann, der in einem **Dorf** wohnte. Dieser Mann war sehr arm, aber er besaß ein **Pferd**, das so exquisit war, das selbst **Könige** es ihm abkaufen wollten- und das zu jedem Preis. Doch der Mann lehnte immer wieder ab. Plötzlich eines Morgens, stellte er fest, dass das Pferd verschwunden war. Alle Menschen aus dem Dorf versammelten um ihr **Mitgefühl** auszudrücken.

Once upon a time there was a poor man living in a village. This man was very poor, but he owned a horse so exquisite that even kings wanted to buy it from him, at any price. But the man refused, again and again. But suddenly, one morning he realized that the horse had disappeared. All the people from the village gathered to express their empathy.

Sie sagten: "Oh, was für ein **Unglück**, was hättest du für ein **Vermögen** mit diesem Pferd verdienen können und man hat dir so viel dafür geboten! Aber du warst zu **dickköpfig** und zu dumm. Jetzt ist das Pferd weg. "

They said, "Oh, what a misfortune, you have earned a fortune with this horse and you were offered so much for it, but unfortunately you were too stubborn and too stupid, now the horse is gone."

Aber der alte Mann lachte nur und sagte: "Ach redet doch keinen **Unsinn**: "Alles was man darüber sagen kann, ist, dass das Pferd jetzt nicht mehr in seinem **Stall** ist. Lass die **Zukunft** kommen und uns zeigen was passiert"

But the old man just laughed and said, "Oh, do not talk nonsense. All that can be said now is that the horse is no longer in his stable. Let the future come and show us what happens.

Nach wenigen Tagen kehrte das Pferd plötzlich zurück in seinen Stall. Nicht nur das, es brachte eine ganze Herde wilder Pferde aus dem Wald mit. Und wieder versammelte sich das ganze Dorf und sie sagten: "Unglaublich, der alte Mann hatte **Recht** sein Pferd ist tatsächlich zurückgekommen, und es hat auch noch ein ganzes **dutzend** toller Pferde mitgebracht. Jetzt kann er so viel Geld verdienen, wie er will." Und sie gingen zu dem alten Mann und sagten: "Oh es tut uns Leid wir konnten das ja nicht voraussehen und die Wege Gottes verstehen, aber du bist unglaublich. Du hast es wohl irgendwie geahnt. Vielleicht kannst du sogar die Zukunft voraussehen."

And then, after a few days, the horse suddenly returned to his stable. And not only that, it brought a whole herd of wild horses out of the forest. And again, the whole village gathered and they said, "Unbelievable, the old man was right, his horse has actually come back, and it has brought back a dozen great horses and now he can make as much money as he wants." And they went to the old man and said, "Oh, sorry, we could not foresee that and understand the ways of God, but you are incredible, you probably guessed, maybe you can even foretell the future."

"So ein **Quatsch**." sagte der alte Mann nur. "Ich weiß nur, eins: Nämlich, dass das Pferd mit einer ganzen Herde Pferde zurückgekommen ist und was morgen geschehen wird, das weiß nur der liebe Gott."

"That's crap," said the old man. "All I know is one thing: the fact that the horse came back with a whole herd of horses and what will happen tomorrow, only God knows."

Und schon ein paar Tage später geschah es, das der einzige Sohn des Mannes, der die neuen Pferde zu**reiten** wollte, dabei vom Pferd fiel. Er **brach** sich dabei seine Beine so schwer, das er fortan wohl nicht mehr würde richtig laufen können. Die Menschen kamen wieder zu dem alten Mann und sagten: "Du hast recht gehabt. Man weiß nie. Die Sache mit den Pferden hat sich als ein **Fluch** erwiesen. Da wäre es besser gewesen, wären die Pferde überhaupt gar nicht erst gekommen. Nun wird dein Sohn ~~für~~ sein ganzes Leben lang **verkrüppelt** sein.

And a few days later, the only son of the man who wanted to ride the new horses fell off his horse. He broke his legs so hard that he could no longer walk properly. People came back to the old man and said, "You were right, you never know, the horse thing turned out to be a curse, so he would have been better if the horses did not return at all. Your son will be crippled for life now.

Aber der alte Mann sagte wieder nur: "Nicht so voreilig. Wartet ab! Man wird sehen was geschieht. Man kann nämlich nur eines darüber sagen, nämlich, dass mein Sohn sich die Beine gebrochen hat. Das ist alles."

But the old man said again, "Don't be to hasty, wait, you'll see what happens, you can only say one thing about it, that my son broke his leg, that's all."

Einige Wochen später ergab es sich das in dem Land ein **Krieg** ausbrach und alle die jungen Männer des Dorfes von der Regierung zwangsweise eingezogen wurden. Nur der Sohn des alten Mannes durfte zu Hause bleiben, weil er für den Krieg **untauglich** war.

A few weeks later, a war broke out in the country and all the village's young men were forcibly conscripted by the government. Only the son of the old man was allowed to stay at home because he was not able to participate.

Und wieder versammelten sich alle Menschen des Dorfes und klagten: "Unsere Söhne sind fort und du hast wenigstens noch deinen Sohn. Er mag zwar seine Beine gebrochen haben, aber er ist bei dir. Unsere Söhne sind fort und der **Feind** ist vielleicht viel mächtiger. Wahrscheinlich werden sie alle sterben. Jetzt werden wir niemanden haben, der sich im Alter um uns kümmert. Aber du hast ja noch deinen Sohn. Er wird bestimmt wieder gesund.

And again all the people of the village gathered and complained, "Our sons are gone, and you have at least your son, he may have broken his leg, but he is with you. Our sons are gone, and the enemy is perhaps much more powerful. Probably they will all die, now we will not have anyone to take care of us in old age, but you still have your son, he's sure to be well again.

Doch der alte Mann sagte wieder nur: "Man kann darüber nur eins sagen: Eure Söhne wurden eingezogen. Mein Sohn ist hier geblieben. Daraus folgt jedoch gar nichts.

But the old man said again: "One can only say one thing about this: your sons were drafted in. My son stayed here, but that does not mean anything."

Zusammenfassung

Ein alter Mann lebte in einem Dorf mit seinem Sohn und hatte ein Pferd. Das Pferd ist eines Tages verschwunden und alle Bewohner haben dem Mann gesagt, dass es besser gewesen wäre, wenn er das Pferd verkauft hätte. Der Mann hörte aber nicht darauf und beklagte sich nicht. Danach kam das Pferd wieder zurück und brachte andere Pferde aus dem Wald mit . Nach ein paar Tagen fiel sein Sohn von einem Pferd und brach sich beide Beine. Die Menschen beurteilten wieder die Situation des Mannes, aber der alte Man hörte wieder nicht darauf. Am Ende brach ein Krieg aus und alle jungen Männer, außer dem Sohn des Mannes, mussten in den Krieg gehen. Wieder kammen die Bewohner zum alten Mann und sprachen darüber wie glücklich er ist, dass sein Sohn zu Hause ist und ihre Kinder im Krieg. Der alte Mann wollte aber nicht viel darüber sprechen, denn man weiß nie, was am nächsten Tag passieren wird.

Summary

An old man lived in a village with his son and had a horse. The horse disappeared one day and all the inhabitants told the man that it would have been better if he had sold the horse. The man does not listen to it and does not complain. Then the horse comes back and brings other horses from the woods. After a few days, his son fell off a horse and broke both his legs. People again judge the man's situation, but the old man does not listen to it. In the end, a war breaks out and all young men, except the son of the man, have to go to war. Again the inhabitants come to the old man and talk about how happy he is, that his son is at home and their children are in a war. The old man does not want to talk much about it, because you never know what will happen the next day.

Wortschatz (Vocabulary)

Dorf - village

Pferd - horse

Könige - kings

Mitgefühl - empathy

Unglück – bad luck

Vermögen - fortune

Dickköpfig - stubborn

Unsinn - nonsense

Stall - stable

Zukunft - future

Recht - right (eg. Human rights)

Dutzend - dozen

Quatsch - crap

Reiten - ride

Fluch - curse

Verkrüppelt - crippled

Krieg - war

Untauglich - disabled

Feind - enemy

Fragen

1. Wie viele Pferde hatte der Mann am Anfang?

2. Mit wem lebte der Mann?

3. Wer kam immer zu dem Mann, um seine Situation zu beurteilen?

4. Was geschach als das Pferd wieder kam?

5. Was passierte mit dem Sohn des Mannes?

6. Was sagen die Bewohner des Dorfes über die Pferde, nachdem sich der Sohn verletzt hat?

a. dass es sich als ein Segen erwiesen hat

b. dass es sich als ein Fluch erwiesen hat

c. es ist einfach sein Schicksal

7. Wie viele Pferde kamen mit dem Pferd des Mannes zurück?

a. zwei

b. zehn

c. ein dutzend

8. Was hat der Sohn gebrochen als er vom Pferd fiel?

a. die Arme

b. beide Beine

c. einen Finger

9. Was sagen die Bewohner, nachdem das Pferd wieder zurück ist?

a. es ist ein magisches Pferd

b. die Pferde sind wunderschön

c. der Mann kann die Zukunft voraussehen

10. Wie endet die Geschichte?

a. die Bewohner klauen das Pferd von dem Mann

b. die Söhne der Bewohner müssen in den Krieg, während der Sohn des Mannes es nicht muss

c. der Mann zieht mit seinem Sohn in ein anderes Dorf und schenkt die Pferde den Bewohnern des Dorfes

Questions

1. How many horses did the man have in the beginning?
2. Who did the man live with?
3. Who would always come to the man to judge his situation?
4. What happened when the horse came back?
5. What happened to the son of the man?
6. What do the villagers say about the horses after their son has been injured?

a. that it turned out to be a blessing

b. that it turned out to be a curse

c. that it's just fate

7. How many horses came back with the man's horse?

a. two

b. ten

c. a dozen

8. What did the son break when he fell off his horse?

a. his arms

b. both legs

c. a finger

9. What do the inhabitants say after the horse returns?

a. it is a magical horse

b. the horses are beautiful

c. the man can foresee the future

10. How does the story end?

a. the inhabitants steal the horse from the man

b. the sons of the inhabitants must go to war, while the son of the man does not have to

c. the man moves with his son to another village and gives the horses to the inhabitants of the village

Antworten

1. Der Mann hatte ein Pferd.

2. Mit seinem Sohn.

3. Die Bewohner aus dem Dorf.

4. Das Pferd kam wieder mit einem Dutzend anderer Pferde.

5. Der Sohn des Mannes fiel vom Pferd.

6. b

7. c

8. b

9. c

10. b

Answers

1. The man had one horse.

2. With his son.

3. The inhabitants of the village.

4. The horse came back with a dozen other horses.

5. The son of the man fell off the horse.

6. b

7. c

8. b

9. c

10. b

Chapter 3 – Der tote Samen (The dead seed)

Ein erfolgreicher **Geschäftsmann** wurde älter und erkannte, dass jemand ihn ersetzen sollte. Anstatt einige seiner Kollegen oder jemanden aus seiner Familie auszuwählen, entschied er sich, etwas Ungewöhnliches zu tun. Er lud alle potenziellen Kandidaten, Finanzdirektoren, Abteilungsleiter, Kassierer, Berater, ein und gab ihnen die folgende Rede:

One successful businessman was getting older and realized that someone should replace him. Instead of choosing some of his colleagues or someone from his family, he decided to do something unusual. He invited all potential candidates, financial directors, chiefs of departments, cashiers, and advisors and gave them the following speech:

"Liebe Freunde, es ist Zeit für mich, mein Geschäft zu beenden und in einen verdienten **Ruhestand** zu gehen. Außerdem ist es jetzt die beste Zeit, einen neuen **Geschäftsführer** auszuwählen, der unser Unternehmen in Zukunft leiten wird ... Ich habe mich entschieden, dass es einer von euch sein wird. "

"Dear friends, it's time for me to finish my business and go to a deserved retirement. Also, now is the best time to choose a new general manager who will lead our company in the future. I decided that it would be one of you. "

Die jungen potenziellen Chefs waren verwirrt ...

The young prospective bosses were confused ...

"Ich werde jedem von euch einen **Samen** geben. Dies ist ein ganz besonderer Samen. Ich will, dass ihr ihn alle pflanzt und **gießt,** und nächstes Jahr wieder zurückbringt, um zu sehen, was ihr damit gemacht habt. Dann werde ich entscheiden, wer der neue Geschäftsführer sein wird. "

"I will give each of you one seed. This is a very special seed. I want all of you to plant it and water it and we will gather again next year to see what you did with it. Then I will decide who will be the new manager. "

Jim war auch bei diesem **Treffen** dabei, und wie auch alle anderen die anwesend waren, bekam er einen Samen. Als er nach Hause kam, teilte er die Nachricht mit seiner Frau und sie beschlossen, den Samen zu nähren, aus dem die **Pflanze** wachsen würde. Sie fanden einen schönen Topf, legten den **Dünger** und einen Thermometer ein, haben ein paar Bücher über Pflanzenanbau gelesen und fuhren mit ihrem Leben fort. Jeden Tag gingen sie zu dem **Topf** und warteten gespannt darauf, dass etwas auftaucht.

Jim was also at this meeting, and as everyone else present, he got the seed, too. When he arrived home, he shared the message with his wife and they decided to nurture the seed from which the plant would grow. They found a nice pot, put the fertilizer, took a thermometer, read a few books on plant cultivation, and continued with their lives. Every day they went to the pot and eagerly waited for something to emerge.

Nach 20 Tagen haben einige von Jims Kollegen bereits angefangen, über ihre wachsenden Pflanzen zu sprechen. Und Jim beobachtete den Topf jeden Tag mit seiner Frau, aber nichts passierte. Es ist über ein Monat vergangen und nichts ist passiert. Über die Pflanzen wurde schon viel diskutiert.

After 20 days, some of Jim's colleagues had already started talking about their growing plants. And Jim watched with his wife every day, but nothing happened. It had been over a month and nothing happened. There had already been a lot of discussion about the plants.

Zur Mittagszeit tauschten sie praktische Ideen über schnellen **Wachstum** aus, und Jim erkannte, dass er als einziger keinen Erfolg hatte.

At lunch-time, they exchanged practical ideas of rapid growth, and Jim realized that he was alone with nothing and that he was unsuccessful.

Sechs Monate später, und es gab immer noch keine Fortschritte. Er begann zu glauben, dass er einen Fehler gemacht hatte. Vielleicht zu viel Wasser oder schlechter Dünger oder etwas anderes, das er nicht erklären konnte. Er wusste, dass er sein Bestes gab und es tat ihm leid, dass er keine Ergebnisse hatte.

Six months later, and there was still no progress. He began to believe that he had made a mistake. Maybe too much water or bad fertilizer or something else that he could not explain. He knew he did the best he could and was sorry he had no results.

Das Jahr ging bald zu Ende, und die jungen Bosse versammelten sich mit ihren Pflanzen, um den Geschäftsführer zu treffen. Jim sagte seiner Frau, dass er den leeren Topf nicht mitnehmen würde, aber sie schaffte es, ihn zu überreden, um den Manager zu erzählen, was passiert war. Er war sehr nervös.

The year soon came to an end, and the young bosses gathered together with their plants to meet the general manager. Jim told his wife that he would not take the empty pot, but she, however, managed to persuade him, telling him to tell the manager fairly what had happened. He was very nervous.

Er dachte, dass dies der unangenehmste Moment für ihn im Leben sein wird. Trotzdem wusste sie, dass sie Recht hatte und war fest davon überzeugt, dass er nichts falsch gemacht hatte. Er nahm seinen Topf mit in den Besprechungsraum. Er sah wunderschöne Pflanzen auf dem Tisch. Sie waren alle groß und ausgewachsen.

He thought that this would be the most unpleasant moment for him in life. Still, she knew she was right and was firmly convinced that there was nothing he did wrong. He took his pot in the meeting room. He saw beautiful plants on the table. They were all big and fully grown.

Er stellte seinen leeren Topf auf den Boden, während andere lachten. Als der Geschäftsführer ankam, schaute er durch alle Pflanzen und begrüßte die Kandidaten. Jim versuchte, so weit von ihm entfernt zu sein, damit er es nicht sehen würde.

He put his empty pot on the floor, while others were laughing. When the general manager arrived, he looked through all the plants and greeted the candidates. Jim tried to be as far away from him, so that he would not see it.

"Wie schön!" sagte der Geschäftsführer. "Ich sehe, dass es jetzt nicht einfach sein wird, einen neuen Manager auszuwählen ..." Und in diesem Moment sah er den leeren Topf. Er hat den Vizepräsidenten gebeten, ihn zu nehmen und den **Eigentümer** zu ihm zu bringen. Jim trat heraus.

"How beautiful!" the general manager said. "I see that it will not be easy to pick a new manager now ..." And, at that moment, he saw the empty pot. He asked the vice president to take it and bring the owner to him. Jim stepped out.

"Oh Gott ... Vielleicht werde ich jetzt rausgeschmissen", dachte er.

"Oh God ... Maybe I'll get kicked out of the company now," he thought.

Als er kam, fragte ihn der Manager, was mit seinem Samen passierte. Und Jim war ganz ehrlich und er entschuldigte sich. Der Manager bat dann alle sich zu sitzen - außer Jim. Er sah sie an und sagte:

When he came, the general manager asked him what happened to his seed. And Jim was all honest and he apologized. The general manager then asked everyone to sit - except for Jim. He looked at them and said:

"Jim, ich bin sehr stolz auf dich ... Jim ist der neue CEO der Firma!"

"Jim, I'm very proud of you. Jim is the new CEO of the company!"

"Nun ... wie ist das möglich? Mein Topf ist leer ...", fragte Jim verwirrt.

"Well ... how is that possible? My pot is empty. " Jim asked confused.

Der alte Manager erklärte: "Vor einem Jahr gab ich jedem von euch einen toten Samen. Es war unmöglich, dass etwas daraus wächst. Jeder von euch, der sah, dass nichts passierte, beschloss es durch gesunde Samen zu ersetzen. Jeder von euch - Außer Jim. Ihr alle habt mir Pflanzen und Blumen gebracht. Nur Jim war stolz auf das **Versagen** und hatte genug **Mut** und Ehrlichkeit, mir einen leeren Topf zu bringen. Ihr wolltet Erfolg - um jeden Preis, und Jims Ehrlichkeit war wichtiger als Erfolg. Deshalb ist er heute der CEO ... "

The old general manager explained: "One year ago I gave each of you a dead seed. It was impossible that something could grow out of it. Each of you, seeing nothing to grow, decided to replace it with healthy seeds. Each of you - except Jim. You all brought me plants and flowers. Only Jim was proud of the failure and had enough courage and honesty to bring me an empty seed. You all wanted success - at all cost, and Jim's honesty was more important than success. That is why he is the CEO today. "

Zusammenfassung

Der Manager einer Firma wollte in Rente gehen und musste deswegen einen neuen Manager auswählen. Er gab den Mitarbeitern einen Samen und sagte ihnen, dass sie sich darum kümmern sollen und nach einem Jahr damit zurückkommen sollen, damit der Manager sieht, was sie mit dem Samen gemacht haben. So wird er den neuen Manager auswählen. Einer der Mitarbeiter, Jim, hatte keinen Erfolg mit dem Samen und nach einem Jahr kam er wieder zurück mit seinem leerem Topf. Alle anderen hatten schöne Pflanzen außer Jim. Nachdem der alte Manager sich die Pflanzen ansah, war er fasziniert. Doch dann sah er Jim's Topf. Er sagte, dass Jim der neue Manager ist. Alle waren geschockt und Jim fragte warum er den Job bekommen hat. Der Manager erklärte, dass er vor einem Jahr jedem von ihnen einen toten Samen gegeben hat. Jeder von den Mitarbeitern hat den Samen durch einen gesunden ersetzt, außer Jim. Deswegen hat Jim gewonnen, weil er ehrlich war und den Manager nicht angelogen hat.

Summary

The manager of a company wanted to retire and therefore had to select a new manager. He gave the staff a seed and told them to take care of it, and after a year they had to come back with it so the manager could see what they had done with the seed. This is how he would pick the new manager. One of the co-workers, Jim, was unsuccessful with the seed and after a year he came back with his empty pot. Everyone else had nice plants except Jim. After the old manager looked at the plants, he was fascinated. But then he saw Jim's pot. He decided that Jim was the new manager. Everyone was shocked and Jim asked why he got the job. The manager explained that a year ago he gave each of them a dead seed. Every worker replaced the seed with a healthy one except for Jim. That's why Jim won, because he was honest and did not lie to the manager.

Wortschatz(Vocabulary)

Geschäftsmann – business man

Ruhestand - retirement

Geschäftsführer - manager

Samen - seed

Gießt (gießen) – to water

Treffen - meeting

Pflanze - plant

Dünger - fertilizer

Topf - pot

Wachstum - growth

Eigentümer - owner

Versagen - failure

Mut – courage

Fragen

1. Warum musste der Geschäftsführer einen neuen Manager auswählen?

2. Wie heißt der Mitarbeiter mit dem leeren Topf?

3. Was gab der Geschäftsführer den Mitarbeitern?

4. Wie lange mussten sich die Mitarbeiter um den Samen kümmern?

5. Wer hat Jim geholfen?

6. Wo hat Jim den Samen aufbewahrt?

a. in dem Kühlschrank

b. unter dem Kissen

c. in einem Topf

7. Warum war Jim nervös?

a. weil er den Samen verloren hat

b. weil jemand den Samen geklaut hat

c. weil der Samen nicht gewachsen ist

8. Wie sahen die Samen von den anderen nach einem Jahr aus?

a. jeder hat einen leeren Topf mitgebracht

b. jeder andere hatte eine schöne Pflanze

c. die Samen waren tot

9. Wer wurde der neue Geschäftsführer?

a. Jim

b. Jim's Frau

c. ein anderer Mitarbeiter

10. Warum war Jims Topf leer?

a. weil der Samen tot war

b. weil Jim den Samen verloren hat

c. weil er sich nicht um den Samen gut gekümmert hat

Questions

1. Why did the manager have to choose a new manager?

2. What is the name of the employee with the empty pot?

3. What did the manager give the employees?

4. How long did the staff have to take care of the seed?

5. Who helped Jim?

6. Where did Jim save the seed?

a. in the fridge

b. under the pillow

c. in a pot

7. Why was Jim nervous?

a. because he lost the seed

b. because someone has stolen the seed

c. because the seed did not grow

8. What did the seeds look like after another year?

a. Everyone brought an empty pot

b. Everyone else had a beautiful plant

c. the seeds were dead

9.Who became the new managing director?

a. Jim

b. Jim's wife

c. other employee

10. Why was Jim's pot empty?

a. because the seed was dead

b. because Jim lost the seed

c. because he did not take good care of the seed

Antworten

1.Weil er in Rente gehen wollte.

2.Jim

3.Einen Samen

4.Ein Jahr lang.

5.Seine Frau

6.c

7.c

8.c

9.b

10.a

Answers

1.Because he wanted to retire.

2. Jim

3. One seed

4. One year

5. His wife

6. c

7. c

8. c

9. b
10. a

Chapter 4 – Ein wahrer Freund (A true friend)

Da war mal ein Junge namens Kevin. Er hatte viele Freunde. Aber was es bedeutet, einen richtigen Freund zu haben, hat er an einem sonnigen Tag gelernt, als er und seine Freunde beschlossen, nach der Schule Fußball zu spielen.

There was a boy named Kevin. He had a lot of friends. But he learned what it means to have a real friend one sunny day when he and his friends decided to play football after school.

Sie alle versammelten sich auf dem **Spielplatz** hinter der Schule. Dort waren seine besten Freunde: Leo, Paul, Mark, Marcus, Tim, Ricky und Willie. Also haben sie sich in zwei Teams aufgeteilt. Kevin landete mit Leo, Paul und Willie in einem Team. Die Sonne schien so stark, dass sie in einem Moment sich kaum sehen konnten.

They all gathered on the playground behind the school. There were all his best friends there: Leo, Paul, Mark, Marcus, Tim, Ricky and Willie. So they divided into two teams. Kevin ended up in the team with Leo, Paul and Willie. The sun was shining so hard that at one point they began to squint and they could hardly see each other.

Und gerade als er sich auf den perfekten **Schuss** vorbereitete, blendete die Sonne ihn mit ihrem **überwältigenden** Glanz. Kevin verfehlte den Ball und er spürte, dass der Boden unter seinen Füßen fiel. Er keuchte in der Luft und fiel mit einem lauten Krachen zu **Boden**. "Dumm, wie konntest du es nicht treffen?" Kevin hörte Willie's **Stimme**, als er versuchte vom Boden aufzustehen. Alles tat weh.

And just when he was preparing to make the perfect hit, the sun blinded him with its overwhelming shine. Kevin missed the ball, and he felt as though the ground was falling under his feet. He gasped in the air and with a loud crash fell to the floor. "Dumb, how did you miss it!" Kevin heard Willie's voice as he tried to get up from the floor. Everything hurt.

"Meine **Großmutter** hätte es besser machen können!" Ricky **kicherte.** "Die Sonne hat mich **zum Wanken gebracht**!" Kevin verteidigte sich. "Ja sicher!" Leo lachte auch. Kevin befand sich in mitten der **Vorwürfe**, als er **Schmerzen** im ganzen Körper fühlte, am meisten in seinem Herzen. Er fühlte sich verletzt, weil seine Freunde ihn ausgelacht haben.

"My grandmother would have kicked it right!" Ricky giggled. "The sun shook me!" Kevin defended. "Yeah, sure!" Leo laughed as well. Kevin found himself in the midst of the accusations as pain was in his whole body, and he felt the most in his heart. He was tired of it because his friends were ridiculing him.

Er schaffte es, aufzustehen und mit großen Schmerzen auf die Füße zu kommen. Er sah das rote, leuchtende **Blut** über sein **Knie** fließen. In der **Ferne** sah er Willie und Ricky wie sie seinen Sturz nachahmen und die anderen lachten über die **Vorstellung.**

He managed to stand up to his feet with great pain. He saw the red, shining blood flowing down his knee. In the distance he saw Willie and Ricky imitate his fall and the others laughed at the performance.

Dann kam Marcus besorgt zu ihm und sah ihn an: "Geht es dir gut?" fragte er. Kevin rieb sich leicht den Kopf. "Du weißt, ich glaube nicht, dass sie Recht haben und ich denke, es war ein guter **Versuch**. Du solltest dich nicht von den Meinungen derer stören lassen, die nicht wirklich deine Freunde sind", sagte Marcus leise und half Kevin, sich auf die Bank neben dem Spielplatz zu setzen.

Then Marcus came to him worriedly, looking at him, "Are you okay?" he asked. Kevin rubbed his head slightly. "You know I do not think they're right and I actually think it was a good try. You should not be bothered by the opinions of those who are not really your friends, " Marcus said quietly, helping Kevin to sit on the bench next to the playground.

Dann rief er den anderen Jungs zu, dass sie sich in dieser Halbzeit ausruhen würden. Dann setzte er sich und sagte zu Kevin: "Weißt du, mit solchen Freunden musst du vorsichtig sein. Ich sage nicht, dass du nicht mit ihnen rumhängen sollst, aber du musst den Unterschied zwischen Freunden und echten Freunden kennen. Sonst wirst du dich verletzen!

Then he shouted to the other boys that they would rest this half-time. Then he sat down and said to Kevin: "You know with such friends you need to be careful. I do not say you do not have to hang out with them, but you have to know the difference between friends and real friends. Otherwise it can hurt you! "

Zusammenfassung

Kevin spielte Fußball an einem sonnigen Tag mit seinen besten Freunden. Als Kevin einen Schuss machen wollte, hat ihn die Sonne geblendet und er hat den Ball verpasst. Er fiel auf den Boden und hat sich das Knie verletzt. Alle haben ihn ausgelacht außer Marcus. Kevin fühlte sich schlecht und verletzt. Marcus hat ihm geholfen und mit ihm gesprochen. Er hat zu Kevin gesagt, dass er wissen muss, wer seine wahren Freunde sind, denn ansonsten wird er sich wieder verletzen.

Summary

Kevin played football on a sunny day with his best friends. When Kevin wanted to take a shot, the sun blinded him and he missed the ball. He fell to the ground and injured his knee. Everyone laughed at him except Marcus. Kevin felt bad and hurt. Marcus helped him and talked to him. He told Kevin that he needed to know who his true friends were, otherwise he'd hurt himself again.

Wortschatz (Vocabulary)

Spielplatz - playground

Schuss - kick

überwältigenden - overwhelming

Boden - ground

Stimme - voice

Großmutter - grandmother

Ins Wanken bringen - shocked

Vorwürfen - accusations

Schmerzen - pain

Blut - blood

Knie - knee

Ferne - distance

Vorstellung - performance

Versuch – try

kicherte - giggled

Questions

1. Was haben die Jungs gespielt?

2. Wann haben sie gespielt?

3. Wie heißt der Junge der sich verletzt hat?

4. Was passiert mit Kevin?

5. Wer lacht ihn aus?

6. Wer hat gekichert?

a. Willie

b. Marcus

c. Ricky

7.Wer hat Kevin geholfen?

a.Marcus

b.Paul

c.Willie

8.Warum hat Kevin den Ball nicht getroffen?

a. wegen dem Schnee

b.weil ihn die Sonne geblendet hat

c.wegen dem Regen

9.Was tut Kevin weh?

a. der Arm

b.der Finger

c.das Knie

10.Was sagt Marcus zu Kevin?

a.dass er dumm ist

b. dass er blutet

c.dass er wissen muss wer seine wahren Freunde sind

Questions

1.What did the boys play?

2.When did they play?

3. What's the name of the boy who got hurt?

4. What happens to Kevin?

5. Who is laughing at him?

6. Who giggled?

a. Willie

b. Marcus

c. Ricky

7. Who helped Kevin?

a. Marcus

b. Paul

c. Willie

8. Why did not Kevin hit the ball?

a. because of the snow

b. because the sun blinded him

c. because of the rain

9. Where does Kevin feel pain?

a. the arm

b. the finger

c. the knee

10. What does Marcus say to Kevin?

a. that he is stupid

b. that he is bleeding

c. that he needs to know who his true friends are

Antworten

1. Fußball

2. Nach der Schule

3. Kevin

4. Er trifft den Ball nicht und er verletzt sich

5. Seine Freunde

6. c

7. a

8. b

9. c

10. c

Answers

1. Football

2. After school

3. Kevin

4. He does not hit the ball and he gets hurt

5. His friends

6. c

7. a

8. b

9. c

10. c

Chapter 5 – Schalen aus Holz (Wooden bowls)

Ein träger alter Mann lebte mit seinem Sohn, seiner **Schwiegertochter** und seinem vierjährigen **Enkel**. Die Hände des alten Mannes **zitterten**, seine Sicht war schwach und seine Beine dienten ihm nicht sehr gut.

A sluggish old man lived with his son, daughter in law, and four-year-old grandson. The old man's hands shivered, his vision was weak, and his legs did not serve him very well.

Wenn die Familie sich zum Essen an den Tisch setzte, würden die zitternden Hände des Großvaters und die geringe **Sehkraft** das Essen sehr schwierig und unangenehm machen. Das Essen würde vom **Löffel** auf den Boden fallen. Wenn er das Glas heben wollte, würde die Milch auf den Tisch fallen. Sein Sohn und seine Schwiegertochter begannen wütend zu werden. "Wir müssen etwas mit unserem Großvater machen", sagte der Sohn eines Tages. Ich habe genug von der verschütteten Milch, lautem Essen und Essen auf dem Boden. Der Sohn und die Schwiegertochter stellten einen kleinen Tisch in die **Ecke** des Zimmers auf.

When the family would sit down at the table to eat, the grandfather's shaking hands and low vision would make the meal very difficult and unpleasant. The food would fall from the spoon to the floor. If he wanted to get a glass, the milk would go down on the table. His son and daughter in law started to get angry. "We have to do something with our grandfather," said the son one day. I have enough of the spilled milk, loud eating and food on the floor." The son and daughter in law set up a small table in the corner of the room.

Der Großvater aß dort, während der Rest der Familie das Essen genoss. Als der Großvater ein paar **Schalen** zerbrach, wurde sein Essen in einer Holzschale serviert. Wenn die Familie manchmal den Großvater ansah, sahen sie manchmal die Tränen in seinen Augen, wenn er allein da saß. Dennoch, die einzigen Worte, die das junge Paar für ihn hatte, waren Worte der **Wut**, wenn etwas auf den Boden fiel.

The grandfather was eating there, while the rest of the family enjoyed the meal. After the grandfather had broken a few bowls, his food was served in a wooden bowl. When the family looked at the grandfather, they would sometimes see the tears in his eyes as he sat there alone.

Nevertheless, the only words the young couple had for him were words of anger if something fell to the floor.

Der vierjährige Enkel sah **schweigend** zu. Eines Abends vor dem Essen sah sein Vater seinen kleinen Sohn mit Holzstücken spielen. Er fragte ihn: "Was machst du?" Der Junge antwortete: "Oh, ich mache kleine Schalen aus **Holz** für dich und Mutter, damit ihr etwas habt, woraus ihr essen könnt, wenn ich groß bin." Der Junge lächelte und fuhr mit seiner Arbeit fort.

The four-year-old grandson looked in silence. One evening before a meal, his father saw his little son playing with pieces of wood. He asked him, "What are you doing?" The boy replied, "Oh, I'm making small wooden pans for you and mom to have something to eat from when I grow up." The boy smiled and continued with his job.

Die Eltern waren sprachlos, und **Tränen** liefen über ihre **Wangen**. Obwohl sie kein Wort sagten, wussten beide, was jetzt zu tun war. An diesem Abend nahmen sie den alten Mann an der Hand und brachten ihn sanft zu seinem Tisch. Bis zum Ende seines Lebens aß der alte Mann mit seiner Familie. Interessanterweise waren weder Sohn noch Tochter besorgt, wenn Milch verschüttet wurde oder wenn das Essen auf den Boden fiel.

The parents were left speechless and their tears began to run down their cheeks. Although they did not speak a word, they both knew what to do. That evening they took the old man by the hand and gently brought him to his table. By the end of his life, the old man ate with his family. Interestingly, neither son nor daughter were worried when milk was spilled or when the food fell on the floor.

Zusammenfassung

Ein alter Mann lebte mit seinem Sohn, Schwiegertochter und Enkel zusammen. Da der Mann sehr alt war, konnte er nicht leicht essen und trinken und oft fiel ihm das Essen auf den Boden oder er würde Milch verschütten. Dies ärgerte seinen Sohn und Schwiegertochter und deswegen stellten sie einen Tisch in der Ecke für ihn auf. Dort aß er aus Schalen aus Holz, weil er die anderen gebrochen hat. Eines Abends spielte der Enkel mit Holz und der Vater fragte ihn was er macht. Sein Sohn sagt ihm, dass er Schalen aus Holz macht, damit er und seine Mutter diese zum Essen benutzen können, wenn er groß wird. Seine Eltern haben danach verstanden, dass sie den Großvater schlecht behandelt haben und brachten ihn wieder zum Tisch damit er mit seiner Familie zusammen essen kann. Sie haben sich nie wieder über ihn beklagt.

Summary

An old man lived with his son, daughter-in-law and grandson. As the man was very old, he could not easily eat and drink and often the food fell to the ground or he would spill his milk. This annoyed his son and daughter-in-law, so they set up a table in the corner for him. There he ate from wooden bowls because he broke the others. One night the grandson played with wood and the father asked him what he was doing. His son told him that he makes wooden bowls so that he and his mother can use them to eat when he grows up. His parents then understood that they had treated the grandfather badly and brought him back to the table so he could eat together with his family. They never complained about him again.

Wortschatz (Vocabulary)

Schwiegertochter – daughter-in-law

Enkel - grandson

Zitterten - shaking

Sehkraft - sight

Löffel - spoon

Ecke - corner

Schalen - bowls

Wut - anger

Schweigend - silently

Holz - wood

Tränen - tears

Wangen – cheeks

Fragen

1. Mit wem lebte der alte Mann?

2. Was fiel dem Mann auf den Boden?

3. Wer war wütend auf den alten Mann?

4. Was haben die Eltern in der Ecke aufgestellt?

5. Warum haben sie dies gemacht?

6. Woraus aß der Großvater?

a. aus einem Teller

b. aus einer Schale aus Holz

c. aus einem Glas

7. Was sah die Familie in den Augen des alten Mannes?

a. Tränen

b. Wut

c. Liebe

8. Was hat der Mann verschüttet?

a. Saft

b. Wasser

c. Milch

9. Wer hat mit Holz gespielt und eine Schale gemacht?

a. der Enkel

b. die Schwiegertochter

c. der Großvater

10. Was haben die Eltern am Ende gemacht?

a. sie brachten den Großvater wieder zum Tisch

b. sie haben den Großvater aus dem Haus gebracht

c. sie haben Schalen aus Holz gemacht

Questions

1. Who did the old man live with?

2. What fell on the ground?

3. Who was mad at the old man?

4. What did the parents set up in the corner?

5. Why have they done this?

6. From what did the grandfather eat?

a. from a plate

b. from a wooden bowl

c. from a glass

7. What did the family see in the eyes of the old man?

a. Tears

b. Anger

c. Love

8. What did the man spill?

a. Juice

b. Water

c. Milk

9. Who played with wood and made a bowl?

a. the grandson

b. the daughter-in-law

c. the grandfather

10. What did the parents do in the end?

a. They brought the grandfather back to the table

b. They brought the grandfather out of the house

c. They made wooden bowls

Antworten

1. Mit seinem Sohn, Schwiegertochter und Enkel

2. Essen

3. Sein Sohn und Schwiegertochter

4. Einen Tisch für den alten Mann

5. Damit er sie nicht beim Essen stört

6. b

7. a

8. c

9. a

10. a

Answers

1. With his son, daughter-in-law and grandson

2. Food

3. His son and daughter-in-law

4. A table for the old man

5. So that he would not bother them while eating

6. b

7. a

8. c

9. a

10. a

Chapter 6 – Eine Brücke des Friedens (A peaceful bridge)

Es gab einmal zwei Brüder, die auf benachbarten Farmen lebten. Eines Tages begannen sie einen ernsthaften **Streit**. Es war der erste große Streit seit vierzig Jahren, seit sie Seite an Seite lebten, **Werkzeuge** teilten und sich gegenseitig halfen.

There were once two brothers who lived on neighbouring farms and they were starting a serious fight. It was the first big fight for forty years, as they lived side by side, sharing tools and helping each other.

Und dann war die Bindung gebrochen. Alles begann mit einem kleinen **Missverständnis,** das zu einem großen Streit und unhöflichen Worten führte, gefolgt von Wochen im **Schweigen.**

And then the bond was broken. It all started with a little misunderstanding that led to a big quarrel and rude words, followed by weeks in silence.

Eines Morgens **klopfte** jemand an Johns Tür. Er öffnete sie und sah einen Mann mit einem Werkzeugkasten. "Ich suche Arbeit", sagte er. "Vielleicht kann ich hier auf deiner Farm Arbeit finden?"

One morning, someone knocked on John's door. He opened it and saw a man with a tool-box. "I'm looking for a job," he said. "Maybe here on your farm I can find some work?"

"Ja", sagte der ältere Bruder. "Ich weiß, was du für mich tun könntest. Siehst du das Haus auf der anderen Seite des Baches? Hier wohnt mein Nachbar; eigentlich ist er mein jüngerer Bruder. Letzte Woche war eine **Wiese** zwischen uns, aber er hat etwas von dem Fluss her gegraben und jetzt, ist ein **Bach** zwischen uns. Er hat es gemacht, um mich wütend zu machen, aber ich werde mich jetzt rechen ... Du siehst diesen **Stamm** neben der **Scheune**? Ich will, dass du einen zwei Meter langen **Zaun** baust, damit ich ihn und sein Haus nicht mehr sehen kann. "

"Yes," said the older brother. "I know what you could do for me. You see that house on the other side of the stream? This is where my neighbour lives - actually, my younger brother. Last week, there was a meadow between us, but he dug something from the river to here and now there is a stream between us. He did it to make me angry, but I'll get back at him ... You see that trunk by the barn? I want you to make me a two-meter-long fence so I cannot even see him or his house anymore."

Der Mann sagte: "Ich verstehe alles. Geben Sie mir **Nagel** und **Bohrer** und ich werde eien tolle Arbeit machen."

The man said, "I understand everything. Give me a nail and a drill and I will do a great job."

Der ältere Bruder musste in die Stadt gehen, also gab er dem Mann das nötige Material und ging weg. Der Mann arbeitete den ganzen Tag.

The older brother had to go to the city, so he gave the carpenter the necessary material and left. The man worked all day.

Als der ältere Bruder um **Mitternacht** zurückkehrte, beendete der Mann die Arbeit. Er war geschockt! Es gab überhaupt keinen Zaun. Er baute eine **Brücke**, die die beiden **Ufer** des Baches verband. Es war eine schöne Brücke, und von seiner anderen Seite näherte sich sein jüngerer Bruder.

As the elder brother returned at midnight, the carpenter finished the job. He was shocked! There was no fence at all. He made a bridge that connected the two banks of the stream. It was a beautiful bridge, and from his other side, his younger brother approached him.

"Du bist wirklich ein großartiger Mann, da du nach allem, was ich getan habe, die Brücke gebaut hast", sagte der jüngere Bruder.

"You're really a great man when you made the bridge after everything I have done," said the younger brother.

Die Brüder standen jeweils auf ihrer Seite der Brücke, und so machten sie sich langsam auf den Weg und trafen sich in der Mitte. Sie sahen, dass der Man seinen **Werkzeugkasten** aufhob und gehen wollte. "Hey, warte! Bleib ein paar Tage bei uns, es gibt noch viele Dinge, die du tun kannst", sagte der ältere Bruder.

Brothers stood each on their side of the bridge, so they slowly set out to meet each other, settling in the middle. They saw that the worker raised his toolbox and wanted to leave. "Hey, wait! Stay with us for a few days. There are many more things you can do," said the older brother.

"Ich würde es gerne", sagte der Mann, "aber ich muss noch viele Brücken bauen."

"I would love to," said the carpenter, "but I need to build many more bridges."

Zusammenfassung

Zwei Brüder hatten ihre eigenen Farmen und lebten in Frieden. Eines Tages hatten sie einen Streit und der ältere Bruder entschied sich, einen Mann anzustellen, der einen riesigen Zaun baut, damit er die Farm und das Haus seines jüngeren Bruders nicht mehr sehen kann. Der Mann hat gesagt, dass er den Job macht. Als der ältere Bruder am Ende des Tages nach Hause kam, sah er, dass der Mann keinen Zaun, sondern eine Brücke über dem Fluss gemacht hat, der die beiden Farmen teilte. Die zwei Brüder waren erstaunt und bedankten sich bei dem Mann. Danach fragten sie ihn, ob er noch bleiben könnte und weiter für sie arbeitet, doch der Mann sagte, dass er leider gehen muss, da er noch viele andere Brücken bauen muss.

Summary

Two brothers had their own farms and lived in peace. One day they had a fight and the older brother decided to hire a man to build a huge fence so he would not be able to see his younger brother's farm and house. The man said that he would do the work. When the elder brother returned home at the end of the day, he saw that the man had not made a fence, but a bridge over the river that divided the two farms. The two brothers were shocked and thanked the man. Then they asked him if he could stay and continue to work for them, but the man said that unfortunately he had to leave as he had to build many other bridges.

Wortschatz (Vocabulary)

Streit – conflict/argument

Werkzeuge - tools

Missverständnis - misunderstanding

Schweigen - silence

Klopfte - knocked

Wiese - meadow

Bach - stream

Stamm - stem

Scheune - barn

Zaun - fence

Nagel - spike

Bohrer - drill

Mitternacht - midnight

Brücke - bridge

Ufer - shore

Werkzeugkasten – tool-box

Fragen

1. Was hatten die beiden Brüder?

2. Welcher Bruder hat einen Arbeiter eingestellt?

3. Was musste der Arbeiter bauen?

4. Wo ging der ältere Bruder nachdem er mit dem Arbeiter gesprochen hat?

5. Was hat der Arbeiter mitgebracht?

6. Was stand zwischen den Farmen der beiden Brüder?

a. ein Wald

b. ein Fluss

c. ein Spielplatz

7. Was hat der Arbeiter am Ende gebaut?

a. eine Brücke

b. ein Gebäude

c. eine Bank

8. Wie begann der ganze Streit zwischen den Brüdern?

a. sie haben sich jahrelang gestritten

b. mit einem kleinem Missverständnis

c. der jüngere Bruder hat etwas geklaut

9. Was wollte der ältere Bruder bauen?

a. eine Brücke

b. einen Tisch

c. einen Zaun

10. Was hat der Arbeiter am Ende gesagt?

a. dass er noch viele Brücken bauen muss

b. dass er gerne zum Abendessen bleiben wird

c. dass er weiter für die Brüder arbeiten wird

Questions

1. What did the two brothers have?

2. Which brother hired a worker?

3. What did the worker have to build?

4. Where did the older brother go after talking to the worker?

5. What did the worker bring?

6. What stood between the farms of the two brothers?

a. a forest

b. a river

c. a playground

7. What did the worker build in the end?

a. a bridge

b. a building

c. a bank

8. How did the whole fight between the brothers begin?

a. They argued for years

b. with a little misunderstanding

c. the younger brother stole something

9. What did the older brother want to build?

a. a bridge

b. a table

c. a fence

10. What did the worker say in the end?

a. that he still has to build many bridges

b. that he would like to stay for dinner

c. that he will continue to work for the brothers

Antworten

1. Farmen

2. Der ältere Bruder

3. Einen Zaun

4. Er ging in die Stadt

5. Einen Werkzeugkasten

6. b

7. a

8. b

9. c

10. a

Answers

1. Farms

2. The older brother

3. A fence

4. He went to the city

5. A toolbox

6. b

7. a

8. b

9. c

10. a

Chapter 7 – Du bist was du denkst (You are what you think)

Zu Beginn des Schuljahres rief der Direktor einer **Grundschule** drei Lehrer an, und teilte ihnen mit, dass sie im letzten Schuljahr die besten Lehrer waren. Er sagte ihnen dann, dass sie im nächsten **Schuljahr** drei **Abteilungen** unterrichten sollten, die aus 90 der intelligentesten Schüler bestehen. Aber er sagte ihnen, dass es eine **Bedingung** gäbe, und diese ist, dass sie ihren Schülern nichts sagen dürfen, damit sie ihre Eltern oder die Eltern von Kindern aus anderen Abteilungen nicht stören.

At the beginning of the school year, the director of one primary school called three teachers and informed them that they were the best teachers in the last school year. He then told them that in the next school year they should teach three departments that consist of 90 of the most intelligent students. But he told them that there was one condition, and that was to say nothing to their students, so they would not disturb their parents or the parents of children from other departments.

Das Schuljahr begann und kamm zu einem Ende. Am Ende des Jahres war die **Durchschnittsnote** für Schüler dieser drei Klassen viel besser als für andere Klassen in ihrer Schule, und sogar 20 bis 30% ihres Erfolges waren besser als der Durchschnitt aller Schulen in der Gegend.

The school year started and finished. At the end of the year, the average grade for students from these three classes was much better than other classes in their school, and even 20 to 30% of their success was better than the average of all schools in the area.

Als der Direktor die Lehrer fragte, was sie darüber dachten, wie sie es geschafft hatten, sagten sie ihm, dass dies eine wundervolle **Erfahrung** für sie sei, dass ihre Arbeit jedoch dadurch erleichtert wurde, dass sie begabte und erfolgreiche Schüler unterrichteten.

When the director asked the teachers what they thought about it and how they achieved it, they told him that this had been a wonderful experience for them, but that their work was made easier by the fact that they taught gifted and successful students.

Der Direktor sagte zu ihnen: "Lassen Sie mich Ihnen die wahre **Wahrheit** sagen: Sie waren weder begabt noch besonders intelligente Schüler, wie wir Ihnen am Anfang sagten, sondern wählten zufällig 90 Schüler aus, die wir in diesen drei Abteilungen eingesetzt haben.

The director told them: "Let me tell you the true truth: Those were not gifted, nor especially intelligent students, as we told you at the beginning, but a randomly selected 90 students that we deployed into those three departments that you taught.

Die Lehrer waren **verwirrt:** "Haben wir zum Erfolg des Schülers **beigetragen**?"

The teachers were confused: "Well, did we contribute to the students' success?"

Der Direktor sagte ihnen: "Nun lassen Sie mich Ihnen eine andere Wahrheit sagen - ich wählte sie, indem ich die Namen aller Lehrer in der Schule auf ein **Blatt** Papier schrieb, und dann zeigte ich mit meinem Finger auf drei Namen - das waren eure Namen."

The director told them, "Now let me admit to you another truth - I chose you by writing the names of all teachers in the school on a sheet of paper, and then I pointed my finger at three names - these were your names."

"Also, was ist der **Grund?**" fragten sie.

"So what's the reason?" They asked.

„Der Grund dafür war es, dass ihr zunächst den **Standpunkt** vertretet habt, dass ihr erfolgreich sein werdet, basierend auf die Information die euch dazu gebracht hat, so zu denken; also habt ihr das Ergebnis erreicht, auch wenn diese Information nicht korrekt war. Ich wollte euch zeigen, dass ihr das Ergebnis dessen seid, was ihr denkt und glaubt."

"The reason is that you initially had the stance that you will achieve success based on the information that led you to expect extraordinary success, so you have achieved the result, regardless of the fact that this information was incorrect. I wanted to show you that you are the result of what you think and what you are hoping for."

Die Lehrer waren beeindruckt und dankbar für die Lektion, die sie gelernt haben.

The teachers were impressed and thankful for the lesson they'd learned.

Zusammenfassung

In einer Grundschule wählte der Direktor drei Lehrer aus und sagte ihnen, dass sie die besten Lehrer seien und dass sie im nächsten Schuljahr die 90 intelligentesten Schüler unterrichten werden. Er hat sie aber gebeten, nichts darüber zu sagen, damit die anderen Schüler und Eltern sich nicht ärgern. Am Ende des Schuljahres hatten diese Klassen die besten Ergebnisse von allen.

Die Lehrer meinten, dass es viel einfacher war, da sie begabte Schüler unterrichteten. Doch der Direktor verriet ihnen dann ein Geheimnis, und zwar, dass diese Schüler ganz normale Schüler waren und dass er die Lehrer ausgewählt hat, indem er einfach auf drei Namen mit dem Finger zeigte. Die Lehrer waren verwirrt und fragten warum er dies gemacht hat und der Direktor sagte ihnen, dass er ihnen zeigen wollte, wie ihre eigenen Gedanken ihnen helfen können, erfolgreich zu sein.

Summary

In a primary school, the director selected three teachers and told them that they were the best teachers and that they would teach the 90 most intelligent students in the next year. But he asked them not to say anything so that the other students and parents would not get angry. At the end of the school year, these classes had the best results of all. The teachers thought it was a lot easier as they had taught gifted students. But the director had then revealed a secret to them, that these students were ordinary students and that he had selected the teachers by simply pointing at three names with his finger. The teachers were confused and asked why he had done this, and the director told them that he wanted to show them how their own thoughts can help them succeed.

Wortschatz (Vocabulary)

Grundschule – primary school

Schuljahr – school year

Abteilungen - departments

Bedingung - condition

Durschnittsnote – average grade

Erfahrung - experience

Wahrheit - truth

verwirrt - confused

beigetragen - contributed

Blatt - sheet

Grund - reason

Standpunkt - stance

Fragen

1. Wer hat die Lehrer ausgewählt?

2. Wie viele Lehrer wurden ausgewählt?

3. Wie viele Schüler wurden ausgewählt?

4.Was war die Bedingung?

5.Wie lange mussten die Lehrer diese Schüler unterrichten?

6.In wie viele Abteilungen wurden die Schüler geteilt?

a.zwei

b.fünf

c.drei

7.Wie fühlten sich die Lehrer am Ende des Schuljahres?

a.sie waren erschöpft

b.sie waren wütend

c.sie meinten, dass es sehr leicht war, da es begabte Schüler waren

8.Was hat der Direktor ihnen mitgeteilt?

a.dass es keine begabten Schüler waren

b.dass sie keinen guten Job gemacht haben

c.dass die Schüler schlecht sind

9.Was fragten die Lehrer danach?

a.Was der Grund dafür war

b.Ob die Eltern verärgert sind

c.Welche Schüler die besten Ergebnisse hatten

10.Was wollte der Direktor ihnen zeigen?

a. dass sie schlechte Lehrer sind

b.dass ihre Gedanken den Erfolg beeinflussen

c.dass sie manchmal lügen müssen

Questions

1.Who chose the teachers?

2.How many teachers have been selected?

3.How many students were selected?

4.What was the condition?

5.How long did the teachers have to teach these students?

6.In how many departments were the students divided?

a. two

b. five

c. three

7. How did the teachers feel at the end of the school year?

a.They were exhausted

b. They were angry

c. They thought that it was very easy as those were gifted students

8.What did the director tell them?

a. that they were not gifted students

b. that they did not do a good job

c. that the students are bad

9.What did the teachers ask?

a. what was the reason

b. if the parents were upset

c. which students had the best results

10.What did the director want to show them?

a. that they were bad teachers

b. that their thoughts influence success

c. that sometimes you have to lie

Antworten

1.Der Direktor

2.Drei

3.90 Schüler

4. dass die Lehrer nichts zu den Schülern oder Eltern sagen

5.Ein Jahr lang

6.c

7.c

8. a

9. a

10. b

Answers

1. The director

2. Three

3. 90 students

4. That the teachers say nothing to the students or parents

5. One year

6. c

7. c

8. a

9. a

10. b

Chapter 8 – Der Taxifahrer (The taxi driver)

Ich habe vor zwanzig Jahren als **Taxifahrer** gearbeitet. Einmal, mitten in der Nacht, kam ich nach einem Anruf zu einem **Gebäude**, das völlig im **Dunkeln** lag, bis auf ein Licht aus dem Fenster im **Erdgeschoss.**

I worked as a taxi driver twenty years ago. Once, in the middle of the night, I arrived at a call in a building that was completely in the dark except for one light from the window on the ground floor.

Unter diesen **Umständen** würden viele Taxifahrer das **Hupe** nur ein- oder zweimal benutzen, eine Minute warten und dann losfahren. Aber ich sah zu viele arme Leute, die auf Taxis als einzige **Transportmittel** angewiesen waren. Wenn ich die **Gefahr** in der Luft nicht riechen würde, würde ich immer zur Tür gehen. Ein Passagier könnte jemand sein, der meine Hilfe braucht, dachte ich. Also, ging ich zur Tür und klopfte.

Under these circumstances, many taxi drivers would use the horn only once or twice, wait a minute and then drive off. But I saw too many poor people who were dependent on taxis as their only means of transport. If I did not smell the danger in the air, I would always go to the door. A passenger could be someone who needs my help, I thought. So I went to the door and knocked.

"Einen **Augenblick**", sagte eine brüchige, ältere Stimme. Ich hörte etwas auf dem **Boden** ziehen. Die Tür öffnete sich nach einer langen Pause. Vor mir stand eine kleine Frau in ihren Achtzigern. Sie trug ein Kleid mit einem **Muster** und einen Hut, an dem der **Schleier** befestigt war, wie jemand in einem Film aus den 40ern. Neben ihr war ein kleiner Koffer.

"Just a moment," said a brittle, older voice. I heard something pulling on the floor. The door opened after a long pause. In front of me was a small woman in her eighties. She wore a dress with a pattern and a hat on which the veil was attached, like someone from a 40's movie. Next to her was a small suitcase.

Die Wohnung sah aus, als wäre sie jahrelang leer gestanden. Alle **Möbel** waren mit **Laken** bedeckt. Es gab keine Uhren an den **Wänden,** keine kleinen Dinge oder **Geschirr** auf der **Theke.** In der Ecke stand eine **Pappschachtel** voller Fotos und Glaswaren.

The apartment looked like no one had lived in it for years. All the furniture was covered with sheets. There were no clocks on the walls, no small things or dishes on the counter. In the corner was a cardboard box full of photographs and glassware.

"Würden Sie bitte meine Tasche zum Auto bringen" sagte sie. Ich nahm den Koffer zum Taxi, und dann kam ich zurück, um der Frau zu helfen. Sie nahm meine Hand und ging langsam zum Rand des **Bürgersteigs.** Sie dankte mir weiterhin für meine **Freundlichkeit.**

"Would you please take my bag to the car," she said. I took the suitcase to the taxi, and then I came back to help the woman. She took my hand and we walked slowly towards the edge of the sidewalk. She kept on thanking me for my kindness.

"Oh, nichts zu danken", sagte ich ihr. "Ich versuche nur meine Passagiere so zu behandeln, wie ich möchte, dass andere meine Mutter behandeln."

"Oh, no need to thank me," I told her. "I'm just trying to treat my passengers as I would like others to treat my mother."

"Oh, du bist so ein guter Junge", sagte sie. Als wir das Taxi betraten, gab sie mir die Adresse und dann fragte sie mich: "Können wir durch die **Innenstadt** fahren?"

"Oh, you are such a good boy," she said. When we entered the cab, she gave me the address and then she asked me, "Could we go through the city center?"

"Es ist nicht der kürzeste Weg", antwortete ich schnell.

"It's not the shortest way," I replied quickly.

"Das macht nichts", sagte sie. "Ich habe es nicht eilig. Ich bin auf dem Weg ins **Krankenhaus."**

"It does not matter," she said. "I'm not in a hurry. I'm on my way to the hospital. "

Ich schaute in den Spiegel. Ihre Augen glitzerten.

I looked in the mirror. Her eyes glittered.

"Ich habe keine Familie mehr", fuhr sie fort. "Ärzte sagen, ich habe nicht mehr viel Zeit."

"I no longer have any family," she continued. "Doctors say I don't have a lot of time left."

Ich beugte mich vor und drehte den Taxameter um. "Welchen Weg soll ich nehmen?", Fragte ich.

I leaned in and turned down the taximeter. "Which way would you like to go," I asked.

Wir fuhren für die nächsten zwei Stunden durch die Stadt. Sie zeigte mir das Gebäude, in dem sie als Fahrstuhlführerin arbeitete. Wir gingen durch die **Nachbarschaft**, wo sie und ihr **Ehemann** lebten. Sie bat mich, vor einem Möbelgeschäft anzuhalten, das früher ein **Tanzsalon** war, in den sie als Mädchen ging. Manchmal bat sie mich ~~gebeten~~, vor einem Gebäude oder einer Ecke abzubremsen, und sie saß da und schaute in die Dunkelheit, ohne etwas zu sagen. Als der erste Strahl der Sonne am Horizont erschien, sagte sie plötzlich: "Ich bin müde. Lass uns jetzt gehen."

We drove through the city for the next two hours. She showed me the building where she used to work as an elevator operator. We walked through the neighbourhood where she and her husband lived. She asked me to stop in front of a furniture store that used to be a dancing salon where she was going as a girl. Sometimes she would ask me to slow down in front of some building or corner, and she sat staring into the darkness, not saying anything. When the first rays of the sun began to appear on the horizon, she suddenly said: "I'm tired. Let's go now."

Schweigend fuhren wir zu der Adresse, die sie mir gegeben hatte.

In silence we drove to the address she gave me.

Es war ein kleines Gebäude. Als wir anhielten, kamen zwei Männer zum Taxi. Voller Aufmerksamkeit folgten sie jeder **Bewegung**. Sie müssen sie erwartet haben. Ich öffnete den Kofferraum und nahm den kleinen Koffer zur Tür. Die Frau saß schon im **Rollstuhl.**

It was a small building. Two men came to the taxi as soon as we stopped. Full of attention, they followed every movement. They must have expected her. I opened the trunk and took the small suitcase to the door. The woman was already sitting in wheelchairs.

"Wie viel schulde ich dir?", Fragte sie und öffnete ihre **Handtasche.**

"How much do I owe you," she asked, opening her purse.

"Nichts", antwortete ich.

"Nothing," I replied.

"Du musst von etwas leben", antwortete sie.

"You must live from something," she replied.

"Es gibt andere Passagiere."

"There are other passengers."

Fast ohne nachzudenken, beugte ich mich vor und **umarmte** sie.

Almost without thinking, I leaned over and hugged her.

"Du hast einer alten Frau einen glücklichen Moment geschenkt", sagte sie. "Danke."

"You gave an old woman one moment of happiness," she said. "Thank you."

Ich drückte ihre Hand und ging in das neblige **Morgenlicht.** Hinter mir schloss sich die Tür. Es war der **Klang** des Endes eines Lebens.

I squeezed her hand and walked into the foggy morning light. Behind me, the door closed. It was the sound of the end of life.

In dieser Schicht habe ich keine anderen Passagiere mitgenommen. Ich war in meinen **Gedanken** verloren. Und den Rest des Tages sprach ich kaum. Was wäre, wenn die Frau einen wütenden

Fahrer bekommen hätte oder jemanden, der seine **Schicht** beenden wollte? Was, wenn ich mich geweigert hätte, sie mitzunehmen? Wenn ich darüber nachdenke, denke ich, dass es das Wichtigste ist, was ich in meinem Leben getan habe. Wir sind überzeugt, dass sich unser Leben um wichtige Momente dreht. Aber wichtige Momente treffen uns oft **unvorbereitet** - schön verpackt in etwas, das manche als unwichtig bezeichnen würden.

In that shift, I did not take any other passengers. I was lost in my thoughts. And the rest of that day, I barely spoke. What if the woman got an angry driver, or someone who was eager to finish the shift? What if I refused to take her? When I think about it, I think that's the most important thing I've done in my life. We are convinced that we think that our lives revolve around important moments. But important moments often take us unprepared - beautifully packaged in what some would call unimportant.

Zusammenfassung

Ein Taxifahrer erzählt von einer alten Frau, die eines Abends mit ihm durch die Gegend gefahren ist. Sie erzählte ihm, dass sie ~~noch~~ nicht mehr viel Zeit hat und dass sie gerne durch die Stadt fahren möchte, bevor sie ins Krankenhaus geht. Sie haben die ganze Nacht gesprochen und sie hat ihm alle Stellen der Stadt gezeigt, die ihr wichtig waren. Am Ende brachte er sie zum Krankenhaus und verabschiedete sich von ihr. Er wusste, dass er sie nie wiedersehen wird, aber trotzdem war er glücklich, dass er ihre Wünsche erfüllt hat. Er hat gelernt, dass auch solch kleine Gesten für jemanden sehr wichtig sein können.

Summary

A taxi driver tells of an old woman who drove around with him one night. She told him that she did not have much time left and that she would like to drive through the city before she goes to the hospital. They talked the whole night and she showed him all the places in the city that were important to her. In the end he took her to the hospital and said goodbye to her. He knew he would never see her again, but still he was happy that he had fulfilled her wishes. He learned that even such small gestures can be very important for someone else.

Wortschatz (Vocabulary)

Taxifahrer – taxi driver

Gebäude - building

Dunkel – the dark

Erdgeschoss – ground floor

Umständen - circumstances

Hupe - horn

Transportmittel - transport

Gefahr - danger

Augenblick - moment

Boden - floor

Muster - pattern

Schleier - veil

Möbel - furniture

Laken - sheet

Wände - walls

Geschirr - dishes

Theke - counter

Pappschachtel – cardboard box

Bürgersteig - sidewalk

Freundlichkeit - friendliness

Innenstadt – city centre

Krankenhaus - hospital

Nachbarschaft - neighborhood

Ehemann - husband

Tanzsalon – dance studio

Bewegung - movement

Rollstuhl - wheelchair

Handtasche - purse

Umarmte - hugged

Morgenlicht – morning light

Klang - sound

Gedanken - thoughts

Schicht - shift

unvorbereitet – unprepared

Fragen

1. Warum kam der Mann zum Gebäude?

2. Wer hat die Tür geöffnet?

3. Was brachte die alte Frau mit sich?

4. Wie sah die Wohnung aus?

5. Auf welchem Geschoss lebte die Frau?

6. Wo musste die Frau hingehen?

a. in ein Restaurant

b. ins Krankenhaus

c. in die Schule

7. Was haben ihr die Ärzte gesagt?

a. dass ihr sehr wenig Zeit bleibt

b. dass sie gesund ist

c. dass sie schwanger ist

8. Der Taxifahrer war:

a. wütend

b. freundlich

c. verärgert

9. Was hat der Taxifahrer am Ende gemacht?

a. er hat Geld für die Fahrt verlangt

b. er hat ihr einen Brief gegeben

c. er hat sie umarmt

10. Was hat er danach gelernt?

a. dass er ein schlechter Mensch ist

b. dass jeder Moment wichtig sein kann

c. dass alte Menschen nett sind

Questions

1. Why did the man come to the building?

2. Who opened the door?

3. What did the old woman carry?

4. What did the apartment look like?

5. On which floor did the woman live?

6. Where did the woman have to go?

a. to a restaurant

b. to the hospital

c. to the school

7. What did the doctors tell her?

a. that she doesn't have much time left

b. that she is healthy

c. that she is pregnant

8. The taxi driver was:

a. angry

b. friendly

c. annoyed

9. What did the taxi driver do in the end?

a. he demanded money for the ride

b. he gave her a letter

c. he hugged her

10. What did he learn after that?

a. that he is a bad person

b. that every moment can be important

c. that old people are nice

Antworten

1. Weil er einen Anruf bekommen hat.

2. Eine alte Frau

3. Einen Koffer

4. Als ob niemand dort lebt.

5. Auf dem Erdgeschoss

6. b

7. a

8. b

9. c

10. b

Answers

1. Because he got a call.

2. An old woman

3. A suitcase

4. As if nobody lives there

5. On the ground floor

6. b

7. a

8. b

9. c

10. b

Chapter 9 – Julia rettet den Kindergarten (Julia saves the kindergarten)

In einer kleinen Stadt lebte eine junge Frau namens Julia Schmidt. Sie war sehr intelligent und talentiert. Da sie Sozialpädagogik studierte, war sie auf der **Suche** nach einem Job in einem Kindergarten. Julia liebte Kinder, und es war schon immer ihr **Traumjob** gewesen. Deswegen beschloss sie, ihre **Bewerbung** in einem kleinen **Kindergarten** abzugeben und dort ihr Glück zu versuchen. Als sie dort ankam, erwartete sie die Direktorin des Kindergartens und **begrüßte** sie.

In a small town lived a young woman named Julia Schmidt. She was very intelligent and talented. Since she was studying social education, she was looking for a job in a kindergarten. Julia loved children and it had always been her dream job. Therefore, she decided to submit her application in a small kindergarten and try her luck there. When she got there, the director of the kindergarten welcomed her.

Julia war nervös, aber sie wollte den Job. Sie stellte sich vor und hat von ihrer Liebe für Kinder erzählt. Außerdem erwähnte sie, dass sie ein **Praktikum** abgeschlossen hat. Die Direktorin hörte Julia zu, aber am Ende sagte sie:

Julia was nervous, but she wanted the job. She introduced herself and told of her love for children. She also mentioned that she had completed an internship. The director listened to Julia, but in the end she said:

„Liebe Frau Schmidt, sie sind sehr freundlich und alles was Sie mir heute erzählt haben ist wundervoll. Ich bin mir sicher, dass Sie eine gute **Erzieherin** sein würden. Ich kann Sie aber nicht **einstellen**. Es tut mir leid."

"Dear Mrs. Schmidt, you are very friendly and all you have told me today is wonderful. I'm sure you would be a good educator. I cannot hire you. I am sorry."

Julia schaute die Frau nervös an.

Julia looked at the woman nervously.

„Können Sie mir bitte sagen, warum Sie dies nicht machen können"?

"Can you please tell me why?"

Die Direktorin antwortete:

The director replied:

„Ich sehe nicht, dass Sie **Erfahrung** in diesem Job haben. Sie können von ihrer Liebe für Kinder reden, aber ich brauche etwas, was mir wirklich sagt, dass Sie für diese Position gut **ausgebildet** sind. Verstehen Sie mich nicht falsch und nehmen sie meine Worte nicht persönlich, aber Sie werden **wahrscheinlich** noch viel arbeiten, bevor Sie als eine kompetente Erzieherin arbeiten können. Ich könnte Sie als **Betreuerin** einstellen. Das bedeutet, dass Sie auf die Kinder während der Schlafenszeit aufpassen. Eine Erzieherin muss wissen, wie man mit Kindern umgeht und was sie tun dürfen und was nicht. Ich habe das **Gefühl,** dass Sie immer noch **unreif** für diese Position sind."

"I do not see that you have experience in this job. You can talk about your love for children, but I need something that really tells me that you are well educated for this position. Do not get me wrong and do not take my words personally, but you probably will work a lot more before you can work as a competent educator. I could hire you as a caregiver. This means that you take care of the children during bedtime. An educator needs to know how to deal with children and what they are allowed to do and what not. I feel like you are still immature for this position. "

Julia sah die Direktorin mit **Enttäuschung** an. Sie fühlte, dass sie mehr als bereit für solch einen Job ist. Für sie war dies ein sehr harter **Schlag** ins Gesicht.

Julia looked at the director with disappointment. She felt that she was more than ready for such a job. For her, this was a very hard slap in the face.

„Frau Schmidt, es tut mir wirklich leid. Sie sind aber sehr jung. Sie haben noch ihr ganzes Leben vor sich und vielleicht bekommen Sie eines Tages diesen Job. Zurzeit ist dies aber unmöglich für Sie. Ich muss dieses **Gespräch** jetzt zu Ende bringen. Es sind noch andere Kandidaten hier. Viel Glück."

"Mrs. Schmidt, I'm really sorry. But you are very young. You still have a whole life and maybe one day you will get this job. At the moment this is impossible for you. I have to finish this conversation now. There are other candidates here. Good luck."

„Ich verstehe. Danke für Ihre Zeit". Julia hob ihre Tasche auf und ging nach draußen. Sie stieg in den Bus und sie konnte ihre Gefühle nicht kontrollieren. Ihre Wangen waren voller Tränen. Sie fühlte sich **gedemütigt** und hatte keine **Hoffnung** mehr. Monate vergingen und sie wusste nicht, wie es weiter gehen soll. Außerdem gab es keine anderen Kindergärten, weil es nicht viele **Bewohner** in der Stadt gab.

"I understand. Thank you for your time." Julia lifted her bag and went outside. She got on the bus and she could not control her feelings. Her cheeks were full of tears. She felt humiliated and had no hope. Months passed and she did not know what to do next. In addition, there were no other kindergartens because there were not many residents in the city.

Eines Morgens ging Julia mit Ihrem Hund in den Park. Sie setzte sich auf eine Bank und nahm die **Zeitungen** aus der Tasche, die sie auf dem Weg gekauft hatte. Auf der ersten Seite sah sie ein **Bild** des Kindergartens, in dem sie sich beworben hat. In dem Artikel stand, dass die Direktorin den Kindergarten schließen muss, weil sie nicht genug Geld haben, um alles zu finanzieren. Die Erzieher haben schon seit zwei Monaten kein **Gehalt** bekommen und die Eltern der Kinder sind mit ihrer Arbeit unzufrieden.

One morning Julia went to the park with her dog. She sat down on a bench and took out the newspapers she had bought on the way. On the first page, she saw a picture of the kindergarten she had applied for. The article said that the director had to close the kindergarten because they did not have enough money to finance everything. The educators had not received a salary for two months and the parents of the children were dissatisfied with their work.

Julia war geschockt. Sie wusste, dass sie etwas tun muss. Es handelt sich um Kinder, die Erziehung und Liebe brauchen. Julia ging nach Hause und beschloss, alle Sachen, von ihrem Auto bis hin zu den paar wertvollen **Kleinigkeiten** zu verkaufen. Das einzige was sie noch übrig hatte, war ihre **Wohnung**, die fast leer war.

Julia was shocked. She knew she had to do something. These were children who needed education and love. Julia went home and decided to sell everything from her car to the few precious little things she had. The only thing she had left was her apartment, which was almost empty.

Danach ging sie in den Kindergarten und **klopfte** an die Tür der Direktorin.

Then she went to the kindergarten and knocked on the door of the director.

„Guten Tag. Kann ich bitte mit Ihnen sprechen?"

"Good day. Can I speak with you, please?"

Die Direktorin sah erschöpft aus und sah Julia nicht mal an.

The director looked exhausted and did not even look at Julia.

„Seien Sie bitte schnell. Ich habe nicht sehr viel Zeit. Ich muss dieses Büro räumen." – sagte die Direktorin.

"Please be quick. I do not have much time. I have to leave this office," said the director.

„Hier." Julia legte einen großen **Stapel** Geld auf den Tisch.

"Here." Julia put a big stack of money on the table.

Die Direktorin drehte sich zu ihr und sah das Geld.

The director turned to her and saw the money.

„Was ist das?" – fragte sie.

"What's that?" - she asked.

„Ich möchte, dass Sie dieses Geld nehmen und die Kosten decken, die Sie haben. Es kann sicher für einige Monate ~~ausreichen~~. Ich werde bis dann wieder einen Weg finden und dem Kindergarten helfen" – sagte Julia entschlossen.

"I want you to take this money and cover the costs you have. It can certainly be enough for a few months. I will find a way and help the kindergarten until then," said Julia, determined.

Die Direktorin war geschockt. Ihr kamen sogar die Tränen.

The director was shocked. She even cried.

„Wie habe ich das verdient? Ich habe Sie doch vor einigen Monaten abgelehnt und einige Sachen gesagt, die vielleicht zu grob waren."

"How did I deserve that? I refused you a few months ago and said some things that were perhaps too crude. "

„Das ist wahr. Aber mir sind die Kinder wichtig. Manche von ihnen brauchen diesen Kindergarten mehr, als es sie braucht. Deswegen kann ich es nicht zulassen, dass Sie ihn schließen. Geld sollte kein Problem darstellen. Wenn man Kinder liebevoll behandelt und mit ihnen gut umgeht, dann werden die Eltern auch zufrieden sein und weiterhin ihre Kinder in den Kindergarten schicken. Es ist nicht so kompliziert wie Sie denken."

"This is true. But the children are important to me. Some of them need this kindergarten more than it needs them. That's why I cannot let you close it. Money does not have to be a problem. If you treat children well and with love, then the parents will be satisfied and continue to send their children to the kindergarten. It's not as complicated as you think."

Die Direktorin wusste, dass Julia recht hat. Sie sah sie an uns sagte:

The director knew that Julia was right. She looked at her and said:

„Sie haben keine Ahnung, wie dankbar ich bin. Das einzige was ich für sie tun kann, ist sie zu bitten, hier mit mir zu arbeiten. Ich kann ihnen für den Anfang kein großes Gehalt **versprechen**, aber.."

"You have no idea how grateful I am. The only thing I can do for you is to ask you to work here with me. I cannot promise you a big salary for the beginning, but .. "

Julia unterbrach die Direktorin:

Julia interrupted the director:

„Geld ist mir unwichtig. Ich würde gerne hier arbeiten und ich verspreche Ihnen, dass Sie bald wieder aus dieser Situation herauskommen werden."

"Money is unimportant to me. I would like to work here and I promise you that you will get out of this situation soon."

So bekam Julia ihren Traumjob. Ja, die ersten Monate waren hart, aber die Kinder liebten sie. Jeden Tag wuchs die Anzahl der neuen Kinder im Kindergarten und somit auch Julias Liebe für die Kinder.

This is how Julia got her dream job. Yes, the first months were tough, but the kids loved her. The number of new children in the kindergarten grew every day and so did Julia's love for the children.

Zusammenfassung

Julia hatte gerade ihr Studium abgeschlossen und wollte sich für die Position als Erzieherin in dem einzigen Kindergarten in ihrer stadt bewerben. Sie liebte Kinder und wollte den Job sehr. Die Direktorin des Kindergartens gab ihr den Job aber nicht, weil sie meinte Julia hat keine Erfahrung und ist unreif für den Job. Dies war sehr hart für Julia. Eines Tages sah sie aber in der Zeitung, dass die Direktorin den Kindergarten schließen wird, weil es kein Geld mehr gibt und nur wenige Kinder noch da sind. Julia entschloss sich, ihre wertvollen Sachen zu verkaufen und der Direktorin zu helfen. Am Ende war die Direktorin geschockt und hat Julia den Job gegeben. Julia hat den Kindergarten gerettet und jeden Tag kamen neue Kinder, weil sie alle liebten.

Summary

Julia had just completed her studies and wanted to apply for the position of educator in the only kindergarten in her city. She loved children and wanted the job very much. The kindergarten director did not give her the job because she said Julia had no experience and was too immature for the job. This was very hard for Julia. One day, however, she saw in the newspaper that the director had to close the kindergarten because there was no money left and only a few children were still there. Julia decided to sell her precious things and help the director. In the end, the director was shocked and gave Julia the job. Julia saved the kindergarten and every day new children came because they all loved her.

Wortschatz (Vocabulary)

Suche - search

Traumjob – dream job

Bewerbung - application

Kindergarten - kindergarten

begrüßte - greeted

Praktikum - internship

Erzieherin - educator

Einstellen - hire

Erfahrung - experience

ausgebildet - educated

wahrscheinlich - probably

Betreuerin - supervisor

Gefühl - feeling

Unreif - immature

Enttäuschung - dissapointment

Schlag - punch

Gespräch - conversation

gedemütigt - hummiliated

Hoffnung - hope

Bewohner - resident

Zeitungen - newspapers

Bild - photo

Gehalt - salary

Kleinigkeiten – little things

Wohnung - apartment

klopfte - knocked

Stapel - stack

Versprechen – to promise

Fragen

1. Welches Studium hat Julia abgeschlossen?

2. Wo wollte sie sich bewerben?

3. Mit wem hat sie gesprochen?

4. Warum wurde sie abgelehnt?

5. Wo ging Julia mit ihrem Hund?

6. Wie hat Julia die Neuigkeit über den Kindergarten gehört?

a. sie hat er in der Zeitung gelesen

b. ein Freund hat es ihr gesagt

c. die Direktorin hat es ihr mitgeteilt

7. Warum wollte die Direktorin den Kindergarten schließen?

a. weil sie erschöpft war

b. weil sie in eine andere Stadt ziehen musste

c. weil sie es nicht mehr finanzieren konnte

8. Was hat Julia getan?

a. sie hat die Zeitung weggeworfen

b. sie hat ihre wertvollen Sachen verkauft

c. sie hat ihren Hund verkauft

9. Wohin ging Julia mit dem Geld?

a. zum Arzt

b. zu der Direktorin

c. in eine Bank

10. Was passierte am Ende?

a. Julia bekam den Job als Erzieherin

b. die Direktorin hat sie rausgeschmissen

c. Julia kaufte sich ein neues Auto

Questions

1. What studies did Julia complete?

2. Where did she want to apply?

3. Who did she talk to?

4. Why was she rejected?

5. Where did Julia go with her dog?

6. How did Julia hear the news about the kindergarten?

a. she read it in the newspaper

b. a friend told her

c. the director has told her

7. Why did the director want to close the kindergarten?

a. because she was exhausted

b. because she had to move to another city

c. because she could not finance it anymore

8. What did Julia do?

a. She threw the newspaper away

b. She has sold her precious things

c. She sold her dog

9. Where did Julia go with the money?

a. to the doctor

b. to the director

c. in a bank

10. What happened in the end?

a. Julia got the job as an educator

b. the director has kicked her out

c. Julia bought a new car

Antworten

1. Sozialpädagogik

2. In einem Kindergarten

3. Mit der Direktorin

4. Weil sie keine Erfahrung hatte und die Direktorin meinte sie sei unreif

5. In den Park.

6. a

7. c

8. b

9. b

10. a

Answers

1. Social education

2. In a kindergarten

3. With the director

4. Because she had no experience and the director said she was immature

5. In the park.

6. a

7. c

8. b

9. b

10. a

Chapter 10 – Ein wahrer Held (A true hero)

Henry und Lucas waren zwei Jungs, die **nebeneinander** lebten. Als sie noch kleine Kinder waren, haben sie ständig zusammen gespielt und man kann sagen, dass sie sogar beste Freunde waren. Ihre Familien haben sich gut verstanden und waren sehr gute Nachbarn. Doch als die Jungs älter wurden und sie in die **Mittelschule** gehen mussten, haben sich die Dinge ein bisschen geändert. Henry war ein sehr intelligenter Junge und hatte in der Schule immer gute **Noten,** während Lucas einige neue Freunde fand, und die Schule als echte **Qual** empfand. Er hasste die Lehrer und fing an sich schlecht zu benehmen. Für ihn waren seine Freunde und die Partys am wichtigsten.

Henry and Lucas were two boys living side by side. When they were little kids, they played together all the time and you could say they were even best friends. Their families got along well and were very good neighbours. But as the boys got older and they had to go to middle school, things had changed a bit. Henry was a very smart boy and always got good grades at school, while Lucas made some new friends and for him school was a real torture. He hated the teachers and started behaving badly. For him, his friends and parties were most important.

Henry wusste, dass seine **Mitschüler** ihn nicht so sehr mogen. Die Lehrer liebten ihn aber. Dies war auch ein Grund, warum ihn seine **Klassenkameraden** ständig gemobbt haben. Sie machten Henry zum **Aussenseiter.** Die anderen würden ihm ständig neue **Spitznamen** geben und da Lucas seine Popularität nicht aufgeben wollte, hat er Henry auch **schikaniert.** Für Henry war dies aber kein Problem. Er wusste wer er ist und dass dies nicht seine Freunde waren. Er war ein wenig enttäuscht von Lucas, aber trotzdem hatte er seine **Ziele** im Kopf. Er wollte gut in der Schule sein und auch wenn ihn andere nicht akzeptierten, versuchte er ihnen bei **Prüfungen** zu helfen.

Henry knew his classmates did not like him so much. But the teachers loved him. That was one of the reasons his classmates bullied him constantly. They made Henry into a geek. The others would constantly give him new nicknames, and since Lucas did not want to give up his popularity, he bullied Henry as well. For Henry this was not a problem. He knew who he was and that these were not his friends. He was a little disappointed with Lucas, but still he had his goals in mind. He wanted to be good at school and even if others did not accept him, he tried to help them with exams.

Eines Tages kamen sie in die Klasse und Lucas stand vor all seinen Klassenkameraden und sagte:

One day they came to class and Lucas stood in front of all his classmates and said:

„Hey hört mal alle zu! Diesen Freitag habe ich das Haus für mich allein und ich mach eine große Party und ihr sollt alle kommen. Es wird der Hammer, wie immer!"

"Hey, listen everyone! I have the house for myself this Friday. I'll have a big party and you should all come. It will be awesome, as always! "

Alle standen auf und gingen zu Lucas um sich über die Party zu freuen. Sie waren sehr aufgeregt und haben gelacht. Dann wollte Lucas noch etwas sagen:

Everyone got up and went to Lucas to talk about the party. They were very excited and laughed. Then Lucas wanted to say something else:

„Ich habe mich nicht sehr gut **ausgedrückt**. Alle können kommen, außer Henry. Sorry Mann, aber ich habe nicht so viel **Platz**, du weißt schon, oder?" Er lachte und **zwinkerte** seinen Freunden zu.

"I did not express myself very well. Everyone can come, except for Henry. Sorry man, but I do not have that much space, you know, right?" He laughed and winked at his friends.

Henry sah ihn für eine Sekunde an und drehte sich um, um seine Bücher rauszunehmen. Er war es schon gewohnt, dass keiner ihn zu Partys einladen wollte. Deswegen war er auch nicht **überrascht**. Alle lachten und haben ihn wieder **gemobbt.**

Henry looked at him for a second and turned to take out his books. He was used to not getting invited to parties. That's why he was not surprised. Everyone laughed and bullied him again.

Der Tag der Party kam an und alle waren aufgeregt und freuten sich. Henry ging nach der Schule nach Hause und spielte Videospiele. Er konnte schon am **Nachmittag** die laute Musik hören, aber er versuchte, sie zu ignorieren. Es war eine große Party und das Haus war voll.

The day of the party arrived and everyone was excited and happy. Henry went home after school and played video games. He could hear the loud music in the afternoon, but he tried to ignore it. It was a big party and the house was full.

In einem Moment, hörte Henry **Schreie** und laute **Geräusche**. Er stand aber nicht auf, denn er dachte, dass es nur laute Musik und Geschrei von der Party ist. Auf einmal hörte er aber etwas **Merkwürdiges**.

In one moment, Henry heard screams and loud noises. He did not get up because he thought it was just loud music and screaming from the party. Suddenly, he heard something strange.

„Feuer!!!!!!! Oh mein Gott. Schnell!! Hilfeeee!!... FEUER!!" Diese Worte wiederholten sich ständig und alle haben geschrien.

"Fire!!!!!!! Oh my God. Fast!! Heeeelp !! ... FIRE !!" These words kept repeating and everyone was screaming.

Henry ging aus seinem Haus und sah ein Feuer im zweiten Stock von Lucas` Haus. Er sah wie alle ängstlich aus dem Haus ~~ängstlich~~ rannten. Henry rief gleich die **Feuerwehr** ~~gleich~~ an. Alle waren draußen, doch er konnte Lucas nicht sehen.

Henry went out of his house and saw a fire on the second floor in Lucas's house. He saw how everyone in the house ran anxiously. Henry called the fire department immediately. Everyone was outside, but he could not see Lucas.

„Lucas ist im **Badezimmer** eingeschlossen. Er kann nicht raus! Hilfeee! Jemand muss ihn rausholen" – rief ein Mädchen aus der Masse.

"Lucas is trapped in the bathroom. He cannot get out! Heeelp! Someone has to get him out," a girl exclaimed from the crowd.

Henrys Herz klopfte nie schneller. Er musste etwas tun. Henry rannte schnell zu dem Haus und ging rein. Alle waren geschockt und ~~waren~~ in Panik. Er ging die **Treppe** auf und konnte ~~nicht leicht~~ nur schwer atmen. Das Feuer hatte sich schon überall ausgebreitet. Er musste die Tür des Badezimmers aufbrechen und danach ging er rein. Er sah Lucas auf dem Boden. Lucas konnte kaum atmen. Henry hob ihn auf und versuchte Lucas aus dem Haus zu bringen. Es war sehr schwer aber er schaffte es bis zur Haustür. Alle waren geschockt als sie die beiden sahen. Zu dieser Zeit kam auch die Feuerwehr. Zum Glück konnten sie das Feuer schnell löschen. Ein **Feuerwehrmann** ging zu Henry und sagte:

Henry's heart never beat faster. He had to do something. Henry quickly ran to the house and went in. Everyone was shocked and in panic. He came upstairs and could not breathe easily. The fire was already everywhere. He had to break the door of the bathroom and then he went in. He saw Lucas on the floor. Lucas was breathing heavily. Henry lifted him and tried to get Lucas out of the house. It was very hard but he made it to the front door. Everyone was shocked when they saw them. At this time fire department arrived. Luckily they were able to extinguish the fire quickly. A fire-fighter went to Henry and said:

„Du bist ein sehr **mutiger** Junge. Ein wahrer Held. Du warst der einzige, der mutig genug war, um deinem Freund das Leben zu retten. Du hast dein eigenes riskiert. Das ist **unglaublich**."

"You are a very brave boy. A true hero. You were the only one brave enough to save your friend's life. You risked your own. That's incredible."

Henry antwortete:

Henry replied:

„Wir sind keine Freunde, aber wir sind Menschen. Ich würde jedem helfen."

"We are not friends, but we are human. I would help everyone. "

Lucas war erschöpft aber er hat diese Worte gehört.

Lucas was exhausted but he heard those words.

„Henry, ich... ich kann es nicht glauben. Du hast mich gerettet. Wie habe ich das verdient." - fragte Lucas.

"Henry, I ... I cannot believe it. You saved me. How did I earn that?" asked Lucas.

„Du kennst mich Lucas. Auch wenn wir keine Freunde mehr sind, weist du immer noch, dass ich dir immer helfen würde." – antwortete Henry.

"You know me, Lucas. Even though we are no longer friends, you still know that I would always help you," replied Henry.

„Danke.. ich fühle mich so schlecht. Ich und die anderen haben dich immer gemobbt. Das war falsch. Am Ende warst du der einzige, der mich aus dem Feuer geholt hat...Glaubst du, dass wir wieder Freunde sein können? Ich verspreche dir, dass ich dich nie wieder enttäuschen werde. Ich werde nie zulassen, dass dir irgendjemand etwas schlechtes sagt...bitte..ich **vermisse** meinen besten Freund..."

"Thanks .. I feel so bad. Me and the others have always bullied you. That was wrong. In the end, you were the only one who got me out of the fire. Do you think we can be friends again? I promise you that I will never disappoint you again. I'll never let anyone tell you something bad ... please..I miss my best friend ... "

„Wir können es ja versuchen." – Henry zwinkerte und Lucas hatte wieder ein Lächeln auf seinem Gesicht.

"We can try it." Henry winked and Lucas had a smile on his face again.

Und es war auch so. Sie wurden wieder beste Freunde und alle anderen liebten Henry. Sie respektierten ihn für seine **Taten** und Henry war sehr **stolz** darauf.

And it was like that. They became best friends again and everyone else loved Henry. They respected him for his actions and Henry was very proud of it.

Zusammenfassung

Henry und Lucas waren früher beste Freunde und Nachbarn. Als sie in die Mittelschule kamen, änderte sich dies, weil Henry gemobbt wurde. Auch Lucas hat sich den anderen angeschlossen und mobbte Henry jeden Tag. Eines Tages hat Lucas eine Party in seinem Haus veranstaltet und hat alle eingeladen, außer Henry. Doch in einem Moment brach ein Feuer auf der Party aus und alle gingen nach draußen, außer Lucas. Er war im Badezimmer eingeschlossen. Henry hat die Schreie gehört und ging ins Haus. Er hat Lucas aus dem Feuer geholt. Am Ende hat sich Lucas schlecht gefült, weil er Henry gemobbt hat, den er war der einzige, der ihm geholfen hat. Sie wurden danach wieder beste Freunde und alle anderen haben Henry für seine gute Tat respektiert.

Summary

Henry and Lucas used to be best friends and neighbours. When they entered middle school, it changed because Henry was bullied. Lucas also joined the others and bullied Henry every day. One day Lucas had a party in his house and he invited everyone but Henry. But in one moment a fire broke out at the party and everyone went outside, except for Lucas. He was trapped in the bathroom. Henry heard the screams and went into the house. He got Lucas out of the fire. In the end, Lucas felt bad because he bullied Henry, who was the only one who helped him. They then became best friends again and everyone else respected Henry for his good deed.

Wortschatz (Vocabulary)

nebeneinander – side by side

Mittelschule – middle school

Noten - grades

Qual - torture

Mitschüler - classmates

Klassenkameraden - classmates

Aussenseiter - outsider

Spitznamen - nickname

Schikaniert - bullied

Ziele - goals

Prüfungen - exams

ausgedrückt - expressed

Platz - space

zwinkerte - winked

überrascht - surprised

gemobbt - bullied

Nachmittag - afternoon

Schreie - screams

Geräusche - noises

Merkwürdiges - strange

Feuerwehr – fire department

Badezimmer - bathroom

Treppe - stairs

Feuerwehrmann - firefighter

mutig - brave

unglaublich - incredible

vermisse - miss

Taten - actions

Stolz – proud

Fragen

1. Was waren Lucas und Henry früher?

2. Warum haben die Mitschüler Henry gemobbt?

3. Worüber hat Lucas im Klassenzimmer gesprochen?

4. Wen hat Lucas nicht zur Party eingeladen?

5. An welchem Tag fand die Party statt?

6. Was hat Henry gehört?

a. Laute Musik und Schreie

b. Gekicher

c. Eine Gitarre

7. Was passierte auf der Party?

a. alle hatten Spaß

b. ein Feuer brach aus

c. Lucas war betrunken

8. Wo war Lucas als das Feuer ausbrach?

a. draußen

b. im Badezimmer

c. im Schlafzimmer

9.Wer hat Lucas gerettet?

a.der Feuerwehrmann

b.das Mädchen

c.Henry

10.Was passierte am Ende?

a.Lucas und Henry wurden wieder beste Freunde

b.Lucas hat Henry gemobbt

c.Henry war wütend

Questions

1.What were Lucas and Henry earlier?

2. Why did the classmates bully Henry?

3.What did Lucas talk about in the classroom?

4. Who did Lucas not invite to the party?

5. What day did the party take place?

6.What did Henry hear?

a. loud music and screams

b. laugh

c. a guitar

7.What happened at the party?

a. everyone had fun

b. a fire broke out

c. Lucas was drunk

8.Where was Lucas when the fire broke out?

a. outside

b. in the bathroom

c. in the bedroom

9. Who saved Lucas?

a. the firefighter

b. the girl

c. Henry

10. What happened in the end?

a. Lucas and Henry became best friends again

b. Lucas has bullied Henry

c. Henry was angry

Antworten

1. Beste Freunde

2. Weil er gute Noten hatte und die Lehrer ihn liebten

3. Über seine Party

4. Henry

5. Am Freitag

6. a

7. b

8. b

9. c

10. a

Answers

1. Best friends

2. Because he had good grades and the teachers loved him

3. About his party

4. Henry

5. On Friday

6. a

7. b

8. b

9. c

10. a

Conclusion

"Reading educates," they say. And in fact, through regular reading, the vocabulary expands automatically. The more often you are confronted with different words, the easier they become. By the way: if you read texts out loud, words are even easier to go from passive to active vocabulary. With half an hour of reading every day, you get a lot. Once that has become a habit, you will not want to miss it anymore. Why should you read more? The advantages are obvious: reading forms, reading extends your horizons, reading relaxes. And in addition, if you read in your learning language, you even have one more advantage: You learn the language and get a good feeling for sentence structure and vocabulary selection.

Perhaps the most obvious tip for more effective reading is unfortunately also difficult to implement. We all would like to read more, but in everyday life, it's hard to find time. To read every day, it has to become a regular habit. That's difficult at the beginning. Always carry this book with you. Read at a break, on the bus or while waiting for the bus. Also, having a regular time reserved for reading can help a lot. For example, you can read for half an hour every night before sleeping.

This is why we hope that you got all the advantages from reading the stories. You can always come back and read them over again. You'll see for yourself that it gets easier each time. Try to memorize and enjoy the interesting situations where the characters find themselves. Not only will you be better in German, but you'll learn some great life lessons through the stories. And don't forget: It takes time and patience, so don't force yourself and try to have fun while reading!

If you have enjoyed this individual book, can you please leave a review for it?

Click here to leave a review for the book on Amazon

Thanks for your support.

Part 3: German Phrase Book

The Ultimate German Phrase Book for Travelers of Germany, Including Over 1000 Phrases for Accommodations, Eating, Traveling, Shopping, and More

Introduction

The phrases "Ein Bier bitte" (One beer, please) and "Wo ist die Toilette?" (Where is the toilet?) are always good to know. It is definitely enough for a night in a German club. But for a whole journey through Germany, you need a lot more than that.

Have you ever been embarrassed to travel to a country without knowing a word in the local language? A whole new dimension of experiences, on the other hand, opens up for the traveler, when he can talk to the locals in their language! Although most Germans know at least a few words in a foreign language - mostly English, French or Spanish - they would definitely appreciate it if you knew some of the most important phrases in German. Learning languages is certainly not easy, but doable! And we're not talking about learning foreign languages to perfection. Isn't it frustrating, even depressing, when you can not talk to other people on a trip and have to spend every evening alone? And is it even exciting if you can not communicate with the locals? Consider how much interesting information and enriching contacts you are missing! Also, when you know some of the phrases, it's much less stressful and uncomplicated to reserve a hotel, tell the pharmacist about your headache, and order your food. Especially since there are many travel destinations and regions where people don't understand a word in English. And your hands and feet are not always enough for communication.

We have collected the most helpful sentences and phrases that are useful in all possible situations you may find yourself in. It always makes sense to know the most important phrases in the language of your travel destination. By that we mean that you can say who you are, where you come from, and you can ask for the way or the time. In this book, you'll find over 1000 phrases in German with English translations, from greetings and directions to restaurants, shopping and night-life. Don't worry - we made sure that the phrases are simple and easy to understand. Also, you'll learn how to pronounce some letter combinations and words. One thing is sure, you'll definitely be able to communicate with people. Everything you need is right in front of you. This is the solution to your communication problems when you travel to Germany. You can get the phrase you need by using the table of contents that will lead you to the topic you are looking for: bank, bar, shopping, transport, restaurant, and many others. With all this being said, you can pack your bags and enjoy your trip to Germany!

Chapter 1 – Pronunciation

In the German language, pronunciation is one of the things you get better at with time. However, some rules can help you to read unfamiliar words correctly.

The German alphabet has 26 letters of the Latin alphabet plus the special characters ä, ö, ü and ß. But there are also German sounds, which are not represented by a separate, individual character, but by a combination of characters.

These are the consonants:

- ch
- ng
- sch

and the diphthongs:

- au
- ei
- eu / äu

sch is being pronounced as the English "sh" e.g. in short.

ng stands for a nasal and it's the closest to the "n" in enl. "singer." You do not hear a g!

äu and **eu** are pronounced the same. Äu is written when the word is closely related to a word with au, such as "Häute", the plural of Haut (skin). In all other cases, eu is written.

The diphtongs are composed of two vowels, but they are so close together that they make one sound.

ch is being pronounced like:

[x] after a, o, u and au (Bach, doch, Buch, auch)

[ç] after all other vowels, after l, n and r and in the endings -chen and -ig (Bäche, ich, Bücher, echt, Milch, durch, manchmal, Mädchen, einig)

[k] before a, o, u, l, r and s (Chaos, Chor, Chlor, sechs)

The pronunciation of ch can in Singular be different than in the plural! Example: das Buch ([X]), die Bücher ([ç]).

h is pronounced when at the beginning of the word and syllable.

If **h** is an elongation sign, its not being pronounced. [h]: Hund, Hunde | hütte, unter|halten; **h** (mute), long vowel: Drohung, sehen, gehen, ruh

st / sp - at the beginning of the word and syllable **st** is pronounced as "scht" and sp as "schp". (Stein, ver|stecken, Sprache, aus|sprechen, aber Ast [st], Wes|pe [sp] etc.)

b, d, g, s, v - at the word and syllable end b, d, g, s and v are pronounced as [p], [t], [k], [s] and [f]. (ab [p], und [t], Weg|gang [k], Haus|tür [s], positiv [f]).

Length and shortness of vowels

The two English words *shit* and *sheet* differ in pronunciation only by the vowel. Shit is short, sheet long. In the German language, there is a long and a short form of all vowels.

It is important to clearly show the difference between long/short in the accented syllables.

Length can be signaled by the following means:

Doubling the vowel at a, e, and o, e.g. in Saal (hall), See (lake) and Boot (boat).

h as an elongation sign possible after all vowels. The h is then not spoken, but only indicates the length of the vocal. (For example, Ahle (awl), sehen(see), ihr(her), ohne(without), Uhr(watch), nähen(sew), Bühne(stage), Höhe(height).

Long **i** is written as **ie** or in exceptional cases as **ieh** (ziehen(pull), Vieh (cattle), etc.). The e (and the h) are not spoken in this combination, but indicate the length of the i such as in Miete(rent), lieben(love) oder die(the).

These length signs are always correct; that means that these vowels are always long. Unfortunately, not all long vowels are explicitly marked. The a in the Tal(valley) or the o in the Rose(rose) are also long. The spelling offers no direct help here.

But there is a strict rule:

Often (but not always) the vowel is spoken long, if only one root consonant follows it.

Examples:

a in Tag(day)

e in Leben(life): [e:]

ö in stör-t(trouble)

ü in üb-t (practice)

Shortness is signaled by the doubling of the following consonant.

The following vowels are all short:

a in Stall (stable)

e in den (because): [ɛ]

i in Mitte (middle)

o in kommen (come)

u in Tunnel (tunnel)

Not all short vowels are marked as such by doubling the following consonant. However, double consonants always show shortness, except for s, for example, the word Fuß (foot) is pronounced with long u.

In German after a long vowel and diphthong, ß (Eszett) is written. The Eszett indicates that the previous vowel is long.

often (but not always) short, if followed by several consonants.

For example:

a in Last (burden)

e in Herbst (autumn)

i in Tinte (ink)

Chapter 2 – Standard phrases in German

Here is a list of the most important standard phrases of the German language. These are the standard phrases that are being used frequently. We have some everyday words for you as well as phrases you can use when you make small-talk with a stranger or a friend. Basic phrases like "hello, please, thank you," and "goodbye" should be very helpful at the beginning. The list is helpful for both beginners and advanced.

Everyday words

Ja - Yes

Nein - No

Bitte - Please

Danke – Thank you

Entschuldigung – Excuse me

Wie bitte? - Pardon?

Es tut mir leid. - I'm sorry (apologizing for something)

Wo? - Where?

Warum? - Why?

Wann? - When?

Wer? - Who?

Wie? - How?

Hier - Here

Dort – There

Understanding

Ich verstehe. - I understand.

Ich verstehe nicht. – I don't understand.

Bitte sprechen Sie langsam. – Please speak slowly.

Können Sie das bitte wiederholen? – Could you repeat that, please?

Können Sie das bitte aufschreiben? - Could you write that down, please?

Sprechen Sie Englisch? - Do you speak English?

Sprechen Sie Französisch? – Do you speak French?

Sprechen Sie Deutsch? – Do you speak German?

Sprechen Sie Spanisch? – Do you speak Spanish?

Sprechen Sie Italienisch? - Do you speak Italian?

Signs

Geöffnet – open

Geschlossen - closed

Eingang - entrance

Ausgang - exit

Drücken - push

Ziehen - pull

Männer – men

Damen - women

Besetzt - occupied

Frei – vacant

Greeting

-Wie geht's dir? / Wie geht es Ihnen? (formal speech) – Gut. / Ganz gut. / Nicht so gut.

(How are you? / How are you? - Good. / Quite well. / Not so good.)

-Hallo. / Guten Morgen / Guten Tag / Guten Abend

(Hello. / Good morning / Good day / Good evening)

-Tschüss. / Auf Wiedersehen.

(Bye / Goodbye)

-Wie heißt du? – Ich heiße…

(What is your name? - My name is…)

-Woher kommst du? – Ich komme aus…

(Where are you from? - I'm from…)

Saying "Bye"

-Tschüss/ Auf Wiedersehen (formal speech), schönen Tag noch.

(Bye/ Until we meet again, have a nice day.)

-Schönes Wochenende.

(nice weekend)

-Mach's gut. Antwort: Mach's besser. / Du auch.

(Take care. Answer: You too)

-Man sieht sich.

(See you)

- Ciao. (= „Tschau")

 (Ciao)

To apologize to someone / Thank someone

-Entschuldigung.

(Sorry)

-Tut mir leid.

(I am sorry)

-Danke. Vielen Dank.

(Thanks. Thank you very much)

-Gerne. / Gern geschehen. / Keine Ursache.

(Gladly./ You are welcome. /Never mind.)

-Schon gut.

(It's fine.)

Compliments

-Das sieht aber gut aus.

(That looks good.)

-Du bist sehr sympathisch.

(You are very sympathetic.)

-Du siehst wirklich toll aus.

(You look really good.)

-Gute Arbeit!

(Good job!)

-Gut gemacht!

(Well done!)

How are you?

-Wie geht es dir / Ihnen?

(How are you / you?)

-Mir geht's gut.

(I'm fine.)

-Gut und selbst?

(Good and you?)

-Hast du dich in deiner neuen Wohnung gut eingelebt?

(Have you settled in well in your new apartment?)

-Ich fühle mich nicht wohl. (krank)

(I am not feeling well. (Sick))

Asking for opinions and expressing yourself

was meinst du? - what do you think?

ich finde, dass ... - I think that ...

ich hoffe, dass ... - I hope that ...

ich fürchte, dass ... - I'm afraid that ...

meiner Meinung nach ... - in my opinion, ...

ich bin einverstanden - I agree

ich bin nicht einverstanden - I disagree or I don't agree

das ist wahr - that's true

das ist nicht wahr - that's not true

Ich denke schon - I think so

Ich denke nicht - I don't think so

Ich hoffe es - I hope so

Ich hoffe nicht - I hope not

du hast Recht - you're right

du liegst falsch - you're wrong

es macht mir nichts aus - I don't mind

das hängt von dir ab - it's up to you

es kommt darauf an - that depends

das ist interessant - that's interesting

das ist lustig - that's funny

Religion

Bist du religiös? - Are you religious?

Nein, ich bin ... - No, I'm ...

Atheist - an atheist

Agnostiker - agnostic

Welcher Konfession gehörst du an? - What religion are you?

Ich bin ... - I'm a ...

Christ - Christian

Muslim - Muslim

Buddhist - Buddhist

Sikh - Sikh

Hindu - Hindu

Protestant - Protestant

Katholik - Catholic

ich bin Jude - I'm Jewish

Glaubst du an Gott? - Do you believe in God?

Ich glaube an Gott - I believe in God

Ich glaube nicht an Gott - I don't believe in God

Glaubst du an ein Leben nach dem Tod? - Do you believe in life after death?

Glaubst du an Wiedergeburt? - Do you believe in reincarnation?

Gibts es … in der Nähe? - is there a … nearby?

eine Kirche - church

eine Moschee - mosque

eine Synagoge - synagogue

einen Tempel - temple

Traveling by public transport

-Wann fährt die nächste Bahn Richtung Hauptbahnhof?

(When is the next train to the main station?)

-Welches Ticket / welche Preisstufe brauche ich bis [Haltestelle]?

(Which ticket / price level do I need until [stop]?)

-Von welchem Gleis fährt…?

(From which track ...?)

-Der Zug hat 10 Minuten Verspätung.

(The train is 10 minutes late.)

- Ist dieser Platz noch frei?

(Is this seat free?)

Getting to know each other

-Wie heißt du? – Ich heiße…

(What is your name? - My name is…)

-Woher kommst du? – Ich komme aus…

(Where are you from? - I'm from…)

-Was machst du beruflich? – Ich bin…

(What are you doing professionally? - I am…)

-Seit wann bist du in Deutschland?

(Since when are you in Germany?)

- Kennst du …?

(Do you know ...?)

Make an appointment

-Hast du Lust, morgen ins Kino zu gehen?

(Do you want to go to the cinema tomorrow?)

-Lass uns morgen ins Kino gehen.

(Let's go to the cinema tomorrow.)

-Wann treffen wir uns?

(When/At what time are we meeting?)

-Hast du morgen Zeit?

(Do you have time tomorrow?)

-Lass uns nochmal telefonieren…

(Let's talk again (on the phone) ...)

Cursing

-So ein Mist!

(Crap!)

-Och nö! / Oh nein! (First one is slang)

(Oh no!)

-Das darf doch wohl nicht wahr sein!

(This can't be happening!)

Being upset with something/someone

-Das soll wohl doch ein Witz sein?

(That's supposed to be a joke?)

-Spinnst du?

(Are you crazy?)

-Du bist wohl verrückt geworden!

(You must have gone crazy!)

- Das ist eine Unverschämtheit!

(That's an impudence!)

Events and activities

Was interessiert Sie (denn) besonders? - What are you interested in?

Gibt es zur Zeit irgendwelche …? - Are there any … on at the moment?

Ausstellungen - exhibitions

kulturellen Veranstaltungen - cultural events

Sportveranstaltungen - sporting events

Gibt es hier irgendwelche …? - Are there any …?

Ausflüge - excursions

Touren - tours

Tagestouren - day trips

Gibt es hier eine Stadtrundfahrt? - Is there a city tour?

Können Sie uns sagen, was zur Zeit … läuft? - Could you tell us what's on at the …?

im Kino - cinema

im Theater - theatre

in der Konzerthalle - concert hall

in der Oper - opera house

Kann ich hier Karten reservieren? - Can I book tickets here?

Haben Sie Broschüren über/von …? - Do you have any brochures on …?

lokalen Sehenswürdigkeiten - local attractions

Können Sie ein gutes Restaurant empfehlen? - Can you recommend a good restaurant?

Haben Sie… - Do you have a map of the…

einen Stadtplan - city

einen Stadtplan - town

Wo ist …? - Where's the …?

das Stadtzentrum? - city centre

die Kunstgalerie? - art gallery

das Museum? - museum

die Einkaufsstraße - main shopping street

der Markt - market

der Bahnhof - railway station

Womit kommt man am besten in der Stadt herum? - What's the best way of getting around the city?

Wo kann ich ein Auto mieten? - Where can I rent a car?

Chapter 3 – Numbers and Colors

Numbers are everywhere and they are important because of many reasons. When you find yourself somewhere and need to know the time or if you need to tell someone how much something costs, than you will certainly find it helpful.

eins >> one

zwei >> two

drei >> three

vier >> four

fünf >> five

sechs >> six

sieben >> seven

acht >> eight

neun >> nine

zehn >> ten

elf >> eleven

zwölf >> twelve

dreizehn >> thirteen

vierzehn >> fourteen

fünfzehn >> fifteen

sechszehn >> sixteen

seibzehn>> seventeen

achtzehn >> eighteen

neunzehn >> nineteen

zwanzig >> twenty

einundzwanzig >> twenty one

zweiundzwanzig >> twenty two

dreiundzwanzig >> twenty three

dreißig >> thirty

vierzig >> forty

fünfzig >> fifty

sechzig >> sixty

siebzig >> seventy

achtzig >> eighty

neunzig >> ninety

hundert >> one hundred

zweihundert >> two hundred

dreihundert >> three hundred

tausend >> one thousand

zweitausend >> two thousand

eine Million >> one million

eine Billion >> one billion

eine Hälfte >> half

weniger >> less

mehr >> more

Time

jetzt >> now

später >> later

vorher >> before

Morgen >> morning

Nachmittag >> afternoon

Abend >> evening

Nacht >> night

Heute >> today

Gestern >> yesterday

morgen >> tomorrow

diese Woche >> this week

letzte Woche >> last week

nächste Woche >> next week

Time of the day

ein Uhr >> one o'clock AM

zwei Uhr >> two o'clock AM

Mittag >> noon

dreizehn Uhr >> one o'clock PM

vierzehn Uhr >> two o'clock PM

Mitternacht >> midnight

halb eun >> half past eight - häufig auch nur: half eight

Duration

_____ Minute >> _____ minute

_____ Stunde >> _____ hour

_____ Tag >> _____ day

_____ Woche >> _____ week

_____ Monat >> _____ month

_____ Jahr >> _____ year

Days

Sonntag >> Sunday

Montag >> Monday

Dienstag >> Tuesday

Mittwoch >> Wednesday

Donnerstag >> Thursday

Freitag >> Friday

Samstag >> Saturday

Months

Januar >> January

Februar >> February

März >> March

April >> April

Mai >> May

Juni >> June

Juli >> July

August >> August

September >> September

Oktober >> October

November >> November

Dezember >> December

Colors

schwarz >> black

weiss >> white

grau >> grey

rot >> red

blau >> blue

gelb >> yellow

grün >> green

orange >> orange

lila >> purple

braun >> brown

Chapter 4 – Transport

The streets can be complicated sometimes and with all the cars, buses and trains, one gets lost easily. You will probably use public transport to travel, such as the train, subway or bus . Or you may go for a walk and need help reaching your destination. Either way, you should remember a few simple questions to ask for directions, buy tickets, or find your way around. If you can tell people where you want to go, you should find your way with a little luck. Even if you do not understand otherwise, these phrases will help you direct your taxi drivers and get rudimentary advice from people on the street. Here are some of the most important phrases to get you to your destination as soon as possible.

Passport control and customs

Darf ich bitte Ihren Pass sehen? - Could I see your passport, please?

Woher reisen Sie ein? - Where have you travelled from?

Was ist der Grund Ihrer Einreise? - What's the purpose of your visit?

Ich bin auf Urlaub - I'm on holiday.

Ich bin auf Geschäftsreise - I'm on business.

Ich besuche Verwandte - I'm visiting relatives.

Wie lange werden Sie sich im Lande aufhalten? - How long will you be staying?

Wo werden Sie übernachten? - Where will you be staying?

Sie müssen … ausfüllen - You have to fill in this …

diese Einreisekarte - landing card

dieses Einreiseformular - immigration form

Genießen Sie ihren Aufenthalt - Enjoy your stay!

Würden Sie bitte Ihre Tasche aufmachen? - Could you open your bag, please?

Haben Sie etwas zu verzollen? - Do you have anything to declare?

Diese Waren sind zollpflichtig - You have to pay duty on these items.

Bus and Train

Wieviel kostet ein Ticket nach _____? - How much is a ticket to _____?

Eine Fahrkarte nach _____, bitte. - One ticket to _____, please.

Wohin geht dieser Zug/ Bus? - Where does this train/ bus go?

Wo ist der Zug/ Bus nach _____? - Where is the train/ bus to _____?

Hält dieser Zug/ Bus in _____? - Does this train/ bus stop in _____?

Wann fährt der Zug/ Bus nach_____ ? - When does the train/ bus for _____ leave?

Wann wird dieser Zug/ Bus in _____ ankommen? - When will this train/ bus arrive in _____?

Wo befindet sich der Fahrkartenschalter? - Where's the ticket office?

Wo befinden sich die Fahrkartenautomaten? - Where are the ticket machines?

Wann fährt der nächste Bus …? - What time's the next bus to …?

Wann fährt der nächste Zug nach …? - What time's the next train to …?

Kann ich den Fahrschein im Bus kaufen? - Can I buy a ticket on the bus?

Kann ich den Fahrschein im Zug kaufen? - Can I buy a ticket on the train?

Was kostet … nach Frankfurt? - How much is a … to Frankfurt?

Eine einfache Fahrt - Single

Ein Hin- und Rückfahrticket - Return

Eine einfache Fahrt erster Klasse - First class single

Ein Hin- und Rückfahrticket erster Klasse - First class return

Einen Einzelfahrschein für Kinder - Child single

Einen Hin- und Rückfahrschein für Kinder - Child return

Einen Einzelfahrschein für Senioren – Senior citizens' single

Einen Hin- und Rückfahrschein für Senioren - Senior citizens' return

Ist das Ticket außerhalb der Stoßzeiten billiger? - Are there any reductions for off-peak travel?

Wann möchten Sie fahren? - When would you like to travel?

Wann möchten Sie zurückfahren? - When will you be coming back?

Ich hätte gerne einen Hin- und Rückfahrschein nach … , mit Rückfahrt am Sonntag - I'd like a return to …, coming back on Sunday

Welchen Bahnsteig brauche ich für …? - Which platform do I need for …?

Ist dies der richtige Gleis nach …? - Is this the right platform for …?

Wo muss ich nach … umsteigen? - Where do I change for …?

Sie müssen in … umsteigen - You'll need to change at …

Kann ich bitte einen Fahrplan haben? - Can I have a timetable, please?

Wie oft fahren die Busse …? - How often do the buses run to …?

Wie oft fahren die Züge …? - How often do the trains run to …?

Ich möchte gern meinen Saisonfahrschein erneuern - I'd like to renew my season ticket, please.

Der Zug hat Verspätung - The train's running late.

Der Zug wurde gestrichen - The train's been cancelled.

Hält dieser Bus …? - Does this bus stop at …?

Hält dieser Zug …? - Does this train stop at …?

Könnten Sie das in den Laderaum legen, bitte? - Could I put this in the hold, please?

Könnten Sie mir sagen, wann wir … ankommen? - Could you tell me when we get to …?

Könnten Sie bitte … anhalten? - Could you please stop at …?

Macht es Ihnen etwas aus, wenn ich mich hier hinsetze? - Do you mind if I sit here?

Die Fahrscheine bitte - Tickets, please.

Alle Fahrscheine und Bahnkarten bitte - All tickets and railcards, please.

Darf ich bitte Ihren Fahrschein sehen? - Could I see your ticket, please?

Ich habe meinen Fahrschein verloren - I've lost my ticket.

Wann kommen wir in … an? - What time do we arrive in …?

Welche Haltestelle ist das hier? - What's this stop?

Welche ist die nächste Haltstelle? - What's the next stop?

Das ist meine Haltestelle - This is my stop.

Ich steige hier aus - I'm getting off here.

Gibt es einen Speisewagen im Zug? - Is there a buffet car on the train?

Stört es Sie, wenn ich das Fenster aufmache? - Do you mind if I open the window?

Dieser Zug endet hier - This train terminates here.

Alle Passagiere bitte aussteigen! - All change, please.

Vergessen Sie bitte nicht Ihr Gepäck - Please take all your luggage and personal belongings with you.

Wieviele Haltestellen sind es bis … - How many stops is it to …?

Ich möchte bitte eine Tageskarte - I'd like a Day Travelcard, please.

Für welche Zonen? - Which zones?

Direction

Wie komme ich zu _____ ? How do I get to _____ ?

...zum Bahnhof? ...the train station?

...zur Bushaltestelle? ...the bus station?

...zum Flughafen? ...the airport?

...zum Stadtzentrum? ...downtown?

...zur Jugendherberge? ...the hostel?

...zum _____ Hotel? ...the _____ hotel?

...zur amerikanischen/ kanadischen/ australischen/ britischenBotschaft? ...the American/ Canadian/ Australian/ British consulate?

...zur deutschen/ österreichischen/ schweizer Botschaft? ...the German/ Austrian/ Swiss consulate?

Wo gibt es viele... Where are there a lot of...

...Hotels? ...hotels?

...Restaurants? ...restaurants?

...Bars? ...bars?

...Sehenswürdigkeiten? ...sights to see?

Könnten Sie es mir auf der Karte zeigen? Can you show me on the map?

Straße - street

Nach links drehen/ abbiegen. - Turn left.

Nach rechts drehen/ abbiegen. - Turn right.

links - left

rechts - right

geradeaus - straight ahead

folgen _____ - towards the _____

nach der _____ - past the _____

vor der _____ - before the _____

Nach _____ schauen. - Watch for the _____.

Norden - north

Süden - south

Osten - east

Westen - west

oberhalb – uphill/above

unterhalb – downhill/below

Taxi

Taxi! - Taxi!

Fahren Sie mich bitte nach _____. - Take me to _____, please.

Wieviel kostet es nach _____ zu fahren? - How much does it cost to get to _____?

Bringen Sie mich bitte dort hin.- Take me there, please.

Wie lange dauert es bis dahin? - How long will the journey take?

Stört es Sie, wenn ich das Fenster aufmache? - Do you mind if I open the window?

Stört es Sie, wenn ich das Fenster zumache? - Do you mind if I close the window?

Sind wir bald da? - Are we almost there?

Wieviel kostet das? - How much is it?

Haben Sie es ein bisschen kleiner? - Have you got this in a smaller size?

Danke, der Rest ist für Sie - That's fine, keep the change.

Möchten Sie eine Rechnung/ einen Beleg? - Would you like a receipt?

Kann ich bitte einen Beleghaben? - Could I have a receipt, please?

Können Sie mich hier um … abholen? - Could you pick me up here at … (time)?

Können Sie hier auf mich warten? - Could you wait for me here?

Wo sind Sie? – Where are you?

Wie lautet die Adresse? - What's the address?

Ich bin ... - I'm ...

im Metropolitan Hotel - at the Metropolitan Hotel

am Bahnhof - at the train station

Wie lautet Ihr Name, bitte? - Could I take your name, please?

Wie lange muss ich warten? - How long will I have to wait?

Wie lange dauert es? - How long will it be?

Es ist auf dem Weg - It's on its way.

Wohin möchten Sie? - Where would you like to go?

Ich möchte ... - I'd like to go to ...

zum Bahnhof – to the train station

Können Sie mich ... bringen - Could you take me to ...?

zum Stadtzentrum - the city centre

Wie viel würde es ... kosten? - How much would it cost to ...?

zum Flughafen – the airport

Könnten wir an einem Bankautomat anhalten? - Could we stop at a cashpoint?

Ist das Taximeter eingeschaltet? - Is the meter switched on?

Bitte schalten Sie das Taximeter ein - Please switch the meter on.

Boat

Wann fährt das nächste Schiff nach ...? - What time's the next boat to ...?

Ich möchte bitte eine ...Kabine - I'd like a ... cabin

Zweier-Kabine - two-berth

Vierer-Kabine - four-berth

Wir brauchen keine Kabine - We don't need a cabin

Ich möchte bitte ein Ticket für ein Auto und zwei Passagiere - I'd like a ticket for a car and two passengers.

Ich möchte bitte ein Fußgängerticket - I'd like a ticket for a foot passenger.

Wie lange dauert die Überfahrt? - How long does the crossing take?

Wann kommt die Fähre in ... an? - What time does the ferry arrive in ...?

Wie lange müssen wir vor der Abfahrt da sein? - How soon before the departure time do we have to arrive?

Wo ist der Informationsschalter? - Where's the information desk?

Wo ist die Kabinennummer …? - Where's cabin number …?

Auf welchem Deck ist/befindet sich …? - Which deck's the … on?

das Büffet - buffet

das Restaurant - restaurant

die Bar - bar

der Laden - shop

das Kino – cinema

Ich bin seekrank - I feel seasick.

Der See ist sehr rau - The sea's very rough.

Der See ist ziemlich ruhig - The sea's quite calm.

Wir bitten alle Autofahrer, sich zu ihrem Fahrzeug zu begeben, um von Bord zu gehen - All car passengers, please make your way down to the car decks for disembarkation.

Wir werden unseren Zielhafen in ungefähr 30 Minuten erreichen - We will be arriving in port in approximately 30 minutes' time.

Könnten Sie bitte Ihre Kabinen räumen? - Please vacate your cabins.

Important terms

Timetable - Fahrplan

single -Einzelfahrschein

return -Rückfahrt

platform - Bahnsteig, Bussteig

waiting room - Wartesaal

ticket office - Fahrkartenschalter

seat - Sitz

seat number - Sitznummer

luggage rack - Gepäckablage

first class - erste Klasse

second class - zweite Klasse

ticket inspector - Schaffner, Schaffnerin

ticket collector - Fahrkartenkontrolleur, Fahrkartenkontrolleurin

penalty fare - erhöhtes Beförderungsentgelt

buffet car - Speisewagen

carriage - Waggon

compartment - Abteil

derailment - Entgleisen

express train - Schnellzug

guard - Schaffner, Schaffnerin

level crossing - Bahnübergang

line closure - Streckensperrung

live rail - Stromschiene

railcard - Bahncard

railway line - Bahntrasse

restaurant car - Speisewagen

season ticket - Zeitkarte

signal - Signal

sleeper train - Schlafwagen

station - Bahnhof

railway station - Bahnhof

train station - Bahnhof

stopping service - Eilzug

ticket barrier - Sperre zur Fahrkartenkontrolle

track - Strecke

train - Zug

train crash - Zugunglück

train driver - Zugführer

train fare - Fahrpreis

train journey - Zugreise

travelcard - Mehrfahrtenkarte

Tube station or underground station - U-Bahn-Haltestelle

Tunnel - Tunnel

bus driver - Busfahrer, Busfahrerin

bus fare - Fahrpreis

bus journey - Busreise

bus stop - Bushaltestelle

bus lane - Busspur

bus station - Busbahnhof

conductor - Fahrtbegleiter, Fahrtbegleiterin

inspector - Aufseher, Aufseherin

luggage hold - Gepäckraum

the next stop - nächste Haltestelle

night bus - Nachtbus

request stop - Bedarfshaltestelle

route - Strecke

terminus - Endstation

Chapter 5 – Accommodation

When you arrive to your destination, you need to get into your accommodations. Do you want to book a room, ask for breakfast, or report to the front desk that you have lost your key? Do not worry! Learn only a few words and have the courage to use them, too, and you will be able to quickly understand! These simple phrases will help you out.

Finding accommodation

Wir suchen nach einer Unterkunft - We're looking for accommodation.

Wir brauchen eine Unterkunft - We need somewhere to stay.

Haben Sie eine Liste mit/von …? - Do you have a list of …?

Hotels - Hotels

Pensionen - B&Bs (bed and breakfasts)

Jugendherbergen - youth hostels

Campingplätzen - campsites

Was für eine Art Unterkunft suchen Sie? - What sort of accommodation are you looking for?

Können Sie eine Unterkunft für mich buchen? - Can you book accommodation for me?

Reservation

Darf ich bitte Ihren Pass sehen? - Could I see your passport?

Würden Sie bitte dieses Anmeldeformular ausfüllen? - Could you please fill in this registration form?

Haben Sie ein freies Zimmer? - Do you have any rooms available?

Wie viel kostet ein Zimmer für eine Person/zwei Personen? - How much is a room for one person/two people?

Gibt es im Zimmer... - Does the room come with...

...ein Badezimmer? ...a bathroom?

...ein Telefon? ...a telephone?

...ein TV? ...a TV?

Kann ich das Zimmer zuerst besichtigen? - May I see the room first?

Haben Sie etwas ruhigeres? - Do you have anything quieter?

...kleineres? ...smaller?

...grösseres? ...bigger?

...saubereres? ...cleaner?

...billigeres? ...cheaper?

OK, ich nehme es. - OK, I'll take it.

Ich will _____ Nacht/Nächte bleiben. - I will stay for _____ night.

Können Sie mir ein anderes Hotel empfehlen? - Can you suggest another hotel?

Haben Sie einen Safe? - Do you have a safe?

...Schliessfächer? - ...lockers?

Ist das Frühstück/Abendessen inklusive? - Is breakfast/supper included?

Um welche Zeit ist das Frühstück/Abendessen? - What time is breakfast/supper?

Kann ich das Frühstück bitte aufs Zimmer haben? - Could I have breakfast in my room, please?

Wann schließt die Bar? - What time does the bar close?

Brauchen Sie Hilfe mit Ihrem Gepäck? - Would you like any help with your luggage?

Bitte reinigen Sie mein Zimmer. - Please clean my room.

Können Sie mich um _____ wecken? - Can you wake me at _____?

Ich möchte mich abmelden. - I want to check out.

Wo ist der Aufzug? - Where are the elevators?

Ich glaube, in der Rechnung steckt ein Fehler - I think there's a mistake in this bill.

Wie möchten Sie bezahlen? - How would you like to pay?

Ich zahle … - I'll pay …

per Kreditkarte - by credit card

bar - in cash

Haben Sie die Minibar benutzt? - Have you used the minibar?

Wir haben die Minibar nicht benutzt - We haven't used the minibar.

Kann uns jemand beim Transport des Gepäcks behilflich sein? - Could we have some help bringing our luggage down?

Können wir unser Gepäck hier irgendwo aufbewahren? - Do you have anywhere we could leave our luggage?

Kann ich bitte eine Rechnung/ einen Beleg haben? - Could I have a receipt, please?

Würden Sie mir bitte ein Taxi rufen? - Could you please call me a taxi?

Ich hoffe, Sie hatten einen angenehmen Aufenthalt - I hope you had an enjoyable stay.

Ich habe meinen Aufenthalt hier sehr genossen - I've really enjoyed my stay.

Wir haben unseren Aufenthalt hier sehr genossen - We've really enjoyed our stay.

Camping

Der Campingplatz - Campsite

Das Zelt - Tent

Der Wohnwagen - Caravan

Das Wohnmobil – Motor home

Haben Sie freie Stellplätze? – Do you have any pitches free?

Kann ich neben meinem Stellplatz parken? – Can I park beside the pitch?

Stellplatz mit Stromanschluß – Serviced pitch

Stellplatz ohne Stromanschluß - Unserviced pitch

Stromanschluß – Electrical connection

Wieviel kostet eine Übernachtung? – What is the charge per night?

Wo sind die Duschen? Where are the showers?

Wo kann man Wäsche waschen? – Where are the laundry facilities?

Ist das Trinkwasser? Is this drinking water?

Kann ich eine Gasflasche ausleihen? – Can I borrow a gas cylinder?

Complaints

Ich hätte gerne ein anderes Zimmer. - I would like a different room.

Die Heizung funktioniert nicht. - The heating does not work.

Die Klimaanlage funktioniert nicht. - The air conditioning does not work.

Das Zimmer ist sehr laut. - The room is very noisy.

Das Zimmer riecht komisch.- The room smells bad.

Ich habe um ein Nichtraucherzimmer gebeten. - I requested a non-smoking room.

Ich habe um ein Zimmer mit Ausblick gebeten. - I requested a room with a view.

Der Schlüssel funktioniert nicht. - My key does not work.

Das Fenster lässt sich nicht öffnen.- The window does not open.

Das Zimmer wurde nicht sauber gemacht. - The room has not been cleaned.

Es sind Mäuse/Ratten/Ungeziefer in meinem Zimmer.- There are mice / rats / bugs in the room.

Es gibt kein heißes Wasser. - There is no hot water.

Ich habe keinen Weckruf bekommen. - I did not receive my wake-up call.

Mir wurde zu viel berechnet. - The bill is overcharged.

Mein Nachbar ist zu laut. - My neighbour is too loud.

Important terms

check-in - Anmeldung

check-out - Abmeldung

reservation - Reservierung

vacanct room - freies Zimmer

to book - buchen

to check in - sich anmelden

to check out - sich abmelden

to pay the bill - Rechnung bezahlen

to stay at a hotel - in einem Hotel wohnen

hotel - Hotel

B&B - Zimmer mit Frühstück

Guesthouse - Gasthaus

Hostel - Hostel

Campsite - Campingplatz

single room - Einzelzimmer

double room - Doppelbettzimmer

twin room - Zweibettzimmer

triple room - Dreierzimmer

suite - Suite

air conditioning - Klimaanlage

bath - Badewanne

en-suite bathroom - Nasszelle

internet access - Internet Zugang

minibar - Minibar

safe - Safe

shower - Dusche

bar - Bar

car park - Parkplatz

corridor - Flur

fire escape - Feuerleiter

games room - Spieleraum

gym - Fitnessstudio

laundry service - Wäscheservice

lift - Aufzug

lobby - Lobby

reception - Rezeption

restaurant - Restaurant

room service - Zimmerservice

sauna - Sauna

swimming pool - Schwimmbecken

manager - Manager, Managerin

housekeeper - Reinigungskraft

receptionist - Rezeptionist, Rezeptionistin

room attendant - Zimmerservice

chambermaid - Zimmermädchen

doorman - Pförtner

porter - Portier

fire alarm - Feueralarm

laundry - Wäscherei

room key - Zimmerschlüssel

room number - Zimmernummer

wake-up call - Weckruf

Chapter 6 – Money

When you visit another country and have to deal with different currencies, it's very useful to know how to ask someone for help or for the price of something.

Akzeptieren Sie den amerikanischen/australischen/kanadischen Dollar? - Do you accept American/Australian/Canadian dollars?

Akzeptieren Sie das britische Pfund? - Do you accept British pounds?

Akzeptieren Sie den Euro? - Do you accept Euros?

Akzeptieren Sie Kreditkarten? - Do you accept credit cards?

Können Sie für mich Geld wechseln? - Can you change money for me?

Wo kann ich Geld wechseln? - Where can I get money changed?

Können Sie für mich Travelerchecks wechseln? - Can you change a traveler's check (USA)/ cheque (UK) for me?

Wo kann ich Travelerchecks wechseln? - Where can I get a traveler's check changed?

Wie ist der Wechselkurs? - What is the exchange rate?

Wo gibt es einen Geldautomaten? - Where is an automatic teller machine (ATM) (Amerik.) / cash dispenser (Brit.)?

Chapter 7 – Restaurants and Food

Tasting different foods and trying the local cuisine is certainly one of the best parts of visiting a foreign country. Before you sit down at a local restaurant before a big meal, you should of course take some time to find out how to talk to the waiter or waitress or how to order your dish. Many restaurants offer menus with translation, but if you also want to move beyond the tourist trails, you may have to come to terms with a German menu! Our list with some basic words and sentences will help you. The following phrases offer a great starting point:

Reservation and Ordering

Einen Tisch für eine Person/zwei Personen bitte. >> A table for one person/two people, please.

Könnte ich die Speisekarte haben? >> Can I look at the menu, please?

Kann ich die Küche sehen? >> Can I look in the kitchen?

Gibt es eine Hausspezialität? >> Is there a house specialty?

Gibt es eine lokale Spezialität? >> Is there a local specialty?

Ich bin Vegetarier. >> I'm a vegetarian.

Ich esse kein Schweinefleisch. >> I don't eat pork.

Ich esse kein Rindfleisch. >> I don't eat beef.

Ich esse nur koscheres Essen. >> I only eat kosher food.

Können Sie es fettarm kochen? >> Can you make it "lite," please?

Tagesmenü >> fixed-price meal

von der Karte >> a la carte

Frühstück >> breakfast

Mittagessen >> lunch

Teezeit >> tea

Abendessen >> dinner

Ich möchte _____. >> I would like _____.

Ich möchte Tischservice _____. >> I want a dish containing _____.

Huhn >> chicken

Rind >> beef

Fisch >> fish

Kochschinken >> ham

Wurst >> sausage

Käse >> cheese

Eier >> eggs

Salat >> salad

Gemüse >> vegetables

Früchte >> fruit

Brot >> bread

Toast >> toast

Glasnudeln >> noodles

Nudeln >> pasta

Reis >> rice

Bohnen >> beans

Kartoffel >> potato

Könnte ich ein Glas von_____haben? >> May I have a glass of _____?

Könnte ich eine Schale von _____haben? >> May I have a cup of _____?

Könnte ich eine Flasche von_____haben? >> May I have a bottle of _____?

Kaffee >> coffee

Tee >> tea

Saft >> juice

Mineralwasser >> water

Wasser >> water

Bier >> beer

Rotwein/Weisswein >> red/white wine

Könnte ich einige _____ haben? >> May I have some _____?

Salz >> salt

Schwarzpfeffer >> black pepper

Butter >> butter

Entschuldigung Kellner? >> Excuse me, waiter?

Ich bin fertig. >> I'm finished.

Es war hervorragend. >> It was delicious.

Bitte räumen Sie den Tisch ab. >> Please clear the plates.

Die Rechnung bitte. >> The check, please. / The bill, please/Can we pay, please

Ordering snacks

Haben Sie auch Snacks / Kleinigkeiten zu essen? - Do you have any snacks?

Haben Sie auch Sandwiches / belegte Brote? - Do you have any sandwiches?

Haben Sie auch etwas zu essen? - Do you serve food?

Wann schließt die Küche? - What time does the kitchen close?

Kann man bei Ihnen noch etwas essen? - Are you still serving food?

Eine Tüte (Germany)/Packerl (Austria) Chips, bitte – A packet of crisps, please.

Welche Geschmacksrichtung hätten Sie gern? - What flavour would you like?

Gesalzen - salted

Käse und Zwiebel - Cheese and onion

Salz und Essig - Salt and vinegar

Was für Sandwiches (belegte Brote) haben Sie? - What sort of sandwiches do you have?

Haben Sie auch warme Gerichte? - Do you have any hot food?

Die Tagesgerichte stehen auf der Tafel - Today's specials are on the board.

Wird man am Tisch bedient oder ist hier Selbstbedienung? - Is it table service or self-service?

Was kann ich dir bringen? - What can I get you?

Möchtest du gern etwas essen? - Would you like anything to eat?

Können wir bitte die Karte haben? - Could we see a menu, please?

If you order something in a cafe that accepts takeaway orders, you might be asked:

Zum hier Essen oder zum Mitnehmen? - Eat in or take-away?

Important terms

Fresh - frisch

Mouldy - schimmelig

Off - schlecht

Rotten - verrottet

Stale - alt

Juicy - saftig

Ripe - reif

Unripe - unreif

Tender - zart

Tough - zäh

over-done or over-cooked - verbrannt

under-done - nicht durch

bland - fad

delicious - hervorragend

horrible - schrecklich

poor - schlecht

salty - salzig

sickly sweet - zuckersüß

sweet - süß

sour - sauer

tasty - lecker

spicy or hot - scharf

mild - mild

to bake - backen

to boil - kochen

to fry - fritieren

to grill - grillen

to roast - braten

to steam - dünsten

breakfast - Frühstück

lunch - Mittagessen

tea - Tee

dinner - Abendessen

supper - Nachtmahl

to have breakfast - frühstücken

to have lunch - zu Mittag essen

to have dinner - zu Abend essen

ingredient - Zutat

recipe - Rezept

to cook - kochen

to lay the table or to set the table - den Tisch decken

to clear the table - den Tisch abräumen

to come to the table - sich an den Tisch setzen

to leave the table - den Tisch verlassen

to wipe the table - den Tisch abwischen

to prepare a meal - ein Gericht zubereiten

bar - die Bar

chef - der Koch, die Köchin

booking or reservation - die Reservierung

menu - die Speisekarte

waiter - der Kellner

waitress - die Kellnerin

wine list - die Weinkarte

starter - die Vorspeise

main course - das Hauptgericht

dessert - der Nachtisch

service - die Bedienung

service charge - der Bedienungsaufschlag

tip - das Trinkgeld

Chapter 8 – Bars

You can easily order your favorite drinks in a bar if you use these phrases below!

Ordering drinks

Servieren Sie Alkohol? >> Do you serve alcohol?

Gibt es einen Tischservice? >> Is there table service?

Ein Bier/zwei Biere bitte >> A beer/two beers, please.

Ein Glas Rotwein/Weisswein bitte. >> A glass of red/white wine, please.

Ein Glas bitte. >> A glass, please.

Ein halber Liter bitte. >> A pint, please.

Eine Flasche bitte. >> A bottle, please.

Whiskey >> whisky

Vodka >> vodka

Rum >> rum

Wasser >> water

Soda >> club soda

Tonic Wasser >> tonic water

Orangensaft >> orange juice

Coca Cola >> Coke

Haben Sie Snacks? >> Do you have any bar snacks?

Einen weiteren, bitte. >> One more, please.

Eine neue Runde bitte. >> Another round, please.

Wann schliessen Sie? >> When is closing time?

Was möchtest du trinken? - What would you like to drink?

Was nimmst du? - What are you having?

Was kann ich dir bringen? - What can I get you?

Ich hätte gern …, bitte - I'll have …, please

Ein großes Pils - a pint of lager

Ein großes Halbdunkles - a pint of bitter

Ein Glas Weißwein – A glass of white wine

Ein Glas Rotwein - A glass of red wine

Einen Orangensaft - An orange juice

Einen Kaffee - A coffee

Eine Cola - a Coke

Eine Cola Light - a Diet Coke

Groß oder klein? - Large or small?

Würde Sie es gerne mit Eis haben? - Would you like ice with that?

Kein Eis, bitte. - No ice, please.

Ein wenig, bitte - A little, please.

Eine Menge Eis, bitte - Lots of ice, please

Ein Bier, bitte - A beer, please.

Zwei Bier, bitte - Two beers, please.

Drei Tequilashots, bitte - Three shots of tequila, please.

Werden Sie schon bedient? - Are you already being served?

Danke, wir werden schon bedient - We're being served, thanks.

Der Nächste, bitte! - Who's next?

Welchen Wein hätten Sie gern? - Which wine would you like?

Ich nehme den Hauswein - House wine is fine.

Was für ein Bier möchten Sie haben? - Which beer would you like?

Möchten Sie es vom Fass oder aus der Flasche? - Would you like draught or bottled beer?

Ich nehme das Gleiche, danke - I'll have the same, please.

Für mich nichts, danke - Nothing for me, thanks.

Ich nehme diese hier - I'll get these.

Der Rest ist für Sie! - Keep the change!

Prost! - Cheers!

Wer ist dran mit der Runde? - Whose round is it?

Das ist meine Runde - It's my round.

Das ist deine Runde - It's your round.

Bitte noch ein Bier - Another beer, please.

Bitte noch zwei Bier – Another two beers, please.

Das Gleiche nochmal, bitte - Same again, please.

Schenken Sie noch Getränke aus? - Are you still serving drinks?

Letzte Bestellungen! - Last orders!

Asking for internet and WiFi

Haben Sie hier Internetzugang? - Do you have internet access here?

Haben Sie hier WiFi? – Do you have WiFi here?

Was ist das Passwort für das Internet? - What's the password for the internet?

The day after

Mir geht es gut - I feel fine.

Ich fühle mich furchtbar - I feel terrible.

Ich habe einen Kater - I've got a hangover.

Ich trinke nie wieder etwas! - I'm never going to drink again!

Smoking

Rauchst du?, rauchen Sie? - Do you smoke?

Nein, ich rauche nicht - No, I don't smoke.

Ich habe aufgehört - I've given up.

Stört es dich, wenn ich rauche? - Do you mind if I smoke?

Möchtest du eine Zigarette? - Would you like a cigarette?

Hast du ein Feuerzeug? - Have you got a lighter?

Do not forget to inform yourself beforehand about tipping practices. This is an essential part of a waiter's salary and should not be left out. However, the uses vary from country to country, so you should inform yourself before you travel.

Note: There is a very strong smoking culture in Austria, and as a result, bars and restaurants allow smokers to smoke on the premises. Sometimes there is a separate section for non-smokers, but not always!

Important terms

Cola/coke - Cola

fruit juice - Fruchtsaft

grapefruit juice - Grapefruitsaft

orange juice - Orangensaft

pineapple juice - Ananassaft

tomato juice - Tomatensaft

iced tea - Eistee

lemonade - Limonade

lime cordial - Limettengetränk

milkshake - Milchshake

orange squash - Orangensaftgetränk

pop - Limo

smoothie - Smoothie

squash-Fruchtsaftgetränk

water-Wasser

mineral water-Mineralwasser

still water-stilles Wasser

sparkling water-Sprudelwasser / Wasser mit Kohlensäure

tap water-Leitungswasser

cocoa-Kakao

coffee-Kaffee

black coffee-schwarzer Tee

decaffeinated coffee or decaf coffee-enkoffeinierter Kaffee

fruit tea-Früchtetee

green tea-grüner Tee

herbal tea-Kräutertee

hot chocolate-heiße Schokolade

tea-Tee

tea bag-Teebeutel

strong-stark

weak-schwach

ale-Dunkelbier

beer-Bier

bitter-Magenbitter

cider-Cider, Apfelwein

lager-Pils

shandy-Radler, Alsterwasser

stout-Dunkelbier, Starkbier

wine-Wein

red wine-Rotwein

white wine-Weißwein

rosé-Rosé

sparkling wine-Sekt

champagne-Champagner

martini-Martini

liqueur-Likör

brandy-Branntwein, Weinbrand

gin-Gin

rum-Rum
whisky, whiskey-Whisky
vodka-Wodka
alcohol-Alkohol
aperitif-Aperitif
bar-Theke
barman-Barkeeper
barmaid-Bardame
bartender-Barkeeper
beer glass-Bierglas
beer mat-Bierdeckel
binge drinking-Besäufnis
bottle-Flasche
can-Dose
cocktail-Cocktail
drunk-betrunken
hangover-Kater
pub-Kneipe
sober-nüchtern
spirits-Spirituosen
tipsy-beschwippst, angeheitert
wine glass-Weinglas

Chapter 9 – Shopping

You want to buy a few souvenirs quickly? Or maybe you need to buy groceries? To make shopping quick and problem-free, we have the most important phrases here:

Haben Sie das in meiner Grösse? > Do you have this in my size?

Wieviel kostet das? >> How much is this?

Das ist zu teuer. >> That's too expensive.

Wollen Sie _____ nehmen? >> Would you take _____?

teuer >> expensive

billig >> cheap

Ich kann es mir nicht leisten. >> I can't afford it.

Ich möchte es nicht. >> I don't want it.

Sie betrügen mich. >> You're cheating me.

Ich bin nicht interessiert >> I'm not interested.

OK, ich nehme es. >> OK, I'll take it.

Kann ich eine Tasche haben? >> Can I have a bag?

Versenden sie ? >> Do you ship ?

Haben Sie Übergrössen? >> Do you stock large sizes?

Ich brauche... >> I need...

...Zahnpasta. >> ...toothpaste.

...eine Zahnbürste. >> ...a toothbrush.

...Tampons. >> ...tampons.

...Seife. >> ...soap.

...Shampoo. >> ...shampoo.

...Schmerzmittel. >> ...pain reliever.

...Medizin gegen Erkältungen. >> ...cold medicine.

...Medizin für den Magen. >> ...stomach medicine.

...ein Rasierer. >> ...a razor.

...ein Regenschirm. >> ...an umbrella.

...Sonnencreme. >> ...sun lotion.

...eine Postkarte. >> ...a postcard.

...Briefmarken. >> ... stamps.

...Batterien. >> ...batteries.

...Schreibpapier. >> ...writing paper.

...ein Stift. >> ...a pen.

...englische Bücher. >> ...English-language books.

...eine englische Zeitschrift/Illustrierte. >> ...English-language magazines.

...eine englische Zeitung. <<===>> ...an English-language newspaper.

...ein englisch-X Wörterbuch. <<===>> ...an English-X dictionary.

Making a decision

Wie fühlen sie sich an? - How do they feel?

Sind sie bequem? - Do they feel comfortable?

Es steht Ihnen - It suits you.

Sie stehen Ihnen - They suit you.

Ist das die einzige Farbe, die Sie haben? - Is this the only colour you've got?

Was halten Sie von diesen hier? - What do you think of these?

Sie gefallen mir - I like them.

Sie gefallen mir nicht - I don't like them.

Die Farbe gefällt mir nicht - I don't like the colour.

Woraus sind sie gemacht? - What are these made of?

Kann man sie waschen? - Are these washable?

Nein, sie müssen in die Reinigung - No, they have to be dry-cleaned.

Ich nehme es - I'll take it.

Ich nehme sie - I'll take them.

Ich nehme das - I'll take this.

Ich nehme sie - I'll take these.

Finding products

Können Sie mir bitte sagen, wo … ist? - Could you tell me where the … is?

die Milch - milk

die Brottheke - bread counter

die Fleischabteilung - meat section

die Tiefkühlabteilung - frozen food section

Werden Sie schon bedient? - Are you being served?

Ich hätte gerne … - I'd like …

dieses Stück Käse - that piece of cheese

ein Stück Pizza - a slice of pizza

sechs Scheiben Schinken - six slices of ham

Ein paar Oliven - Some olives

Wieviel hätten Sie gerne? - How much would you like?

300 Gramm - 300 grams

Ein halbes Kilo, bitte - half a kilo

zwei Pfund (450 Gramm) - two pounds

Das macht €32.47 - that's €32.47

Kann ich bitte eine Tüte (Germany)/ ein Sackerl (Austria) haben? - Could I have a carrier bag, please?

Kann ich bitte noch eine Tüte/ ein Sackerl haben? - Could I have another carrier bag, please?

Brauchen Sie Hilfe beim Einpacken? - Do you need any help packing?

Haben Sie eine Kundenkarte? - Do you have a loyalty card?

At a hair salon

Ich hätte gerne einen Haarschnitt, bitte - I'd like a haircut, please.

Muss ich mir einen Termin ausmachen? - Do I need to book?

Kann ich gleich dableiben? - Are you able to see me now?

Möchten Sie gerne einen Termin ausmachen? - Would you like to make an appointment?

Möchten Sie die Haare gewaschen haben? - Would you like me to wash it?

Was möchten Sie? - What would you like?

Wie soll ich es schneiden? - How would you like me to cut it?

Das überlasse ich Ihnen - I'll leave it to you.

Ich hätte gern … - I'd like …

einen Nachschnitt - a trim

einen neuen Style - a new style

eine Dauerwelle - a perm

einen Pony - a fringe

Strähnen - some highlights

eine Färbung - it coloured

Bitte nur nachschneiden - Just a trim, please

Wie kurz hätten Sie es gern? - How short would you like it?

nicht zu kurz - not too short

ziemlich kurz - quite short

sehr kurz - very short

Stufe eins - grade one

Stufe zwei - grade two

Stufe drei - grade three

Stufe vier - grade four

komplett rasiert - completely shaven

Haben Sie einen Scheitel? - Do you have a parting?

Im Nacken gerade, bitte - Square at the back, please

Im Nacken zulaufend, bitte - Tapered at the back, please

Das ist in Ordnung, danke - That's fine, thanks

Welche Farbe möchten Sie? - What colour would you like?

Welche dieser Farben möchten Sie? - Which of these colours would you like?

Möchten Sie es geföhnt? - Would you like it blow-dried?

Können Sie mir bitte den Bart nachschneiden? - Could you trim my beard, please?

Können Sie mir bitte den Schnurrbart nachschneiden? - Could you trim my moustache, please?

Möchten Sie etwas ...? - Would you like anything on it?

Haarwachs - a little wax

Gel - some gel

Haarspray - some hairspray

Nein, danke - Nothing, thanks.

Wieviel bekommen Sie? - How much do I owe you?

Important terms

cheap-billig

customer-Kunde

discount-Rabatt

expensive-teuer

price-Preis

sale-Ausverkauf

shop-Laden

shopping bag-Einkaufstasche

shopping list-Einkaufsliste

special offer-Angebot

to buy-kaufen

to sell-verkaufen

to order-bestellen

to go shopping-einkaufen gehen

Im Laden

aisle-Gang

basket-Korb

counter-Ladentresen

fitting room-Ankleideraum

manager-Filialleiter

shelf-Regal

shop assistant-Ladenverkäufer

shop window-Ladenfenster

stockroom-Lagerraum

trolley-Einkaufswagen

cashier-Kassierer, Kassiererin

cash-Bargeld

change-Kleingeld

checkout-Kasse

complaint-Beschwerde

credit card-Kreditkarte

in stock-auf Lager

out of stock-nicht auf Lager

plastic bag or carrier bag-Plastiktüte

purse-Geldbeutel

queue-Schlange

receipt-Quittung

refund-Rückerstattung

till-Kasse

wallet-Brieftasche

Chapter 10 – Driving

If you plan on driving with your own car or renting one, then you should definitely know some rules and how to get to your destination without any issues. Here are some important phrases:

Könnte ich ein Auto mieten? >> Can I rent a car?

Kann ich eine Versicherung bekommen? >> Can I get insurance?

STOP >> stop

Einbahnstraße >> one way

Vorfahrt beachten >> yield

Parkverbot >> no parking

Höchstgeschwindigkeit >> speed limit

Tankstelle >> gas station /service station station

Benzin >> petrol /gas

Diesel >> diesel

Important terms

bypass-Umgehungsstraße

country lane-Landstraße

dual carriageway-zweispurige Schnellstraße

main road-Bundesstraße

motorway-Autobahn

one-way street-Einbahnstraße

ring road-Ortsumgehung

road-Straße

toll road-mautpflichtige Straße

Straßeneigenschaften

corner-Straßenecke

crossroads-Kreuzung

kerb-Bordstein

fork-Gabelung

hard shoulder-Seitenstreifen

junction-Kreuzung

lay-by-Parkstreifen

level crossing-Bahnübergang

pavement-Bürgersteig

pedestrian crossing-Fußgängerüberweg

road sign-Verkehrszeichen

roadside-Straßenrand

roadworks-Straßenarbeiten

roundabout-Kreisverkehr

services-Autobahnraststätte

signpost-Schild

speed limit-Geschwindigkeitsbegrenzung

T-junction-T-Kreuzung

toll-Maut

traffic light-Ampel

turning-abbiegen

accident-Unfall

breakdown-Panne

breathalyser-Alkoholtest-Röhrchen

jack-Wagenheber

jump leads-Starthilfekabel

flat tyre-Reifenpanne

fog-Nebel

icy road-vereiste Straße

puncture-Panne

speeding fine-Bußgeld wegen Geschwindigkeitsüberschreitung

spray-Spritzwasser

traffic jam-Verkehrsstau

to crash-zusammenstoßen

to have an accident-einen Unfall haben

to skid-rutschen

to stall-Motor abwürgen

to swerve-ausweichen

driving instructor-Fahrlehrer, Fahrlehrerin

driving lesson-Fahrstunde

driving licence-Führerschein

driving school-Fahrschule

driving test-Fahrprüfung

learner driver-Fahrschüler, Fahrschülerin

to fail your driving test- die Fahrprüfung durchfallen

to pass your driving test-die Fahrprüfung bestehen

car park-Parkplatz

disabled parking space-Behindertenparkplatz

multi-storey car park-Parkhaus

to park-parken

parking meter-Parkuhr

parking space-Stellplatz

parking ticket-Strafzettel

traffic warden-Polizeihelfer, Polizeihelferin

car wash-Autowaschstraße

diesel-Diesel

oil-Öl

petrol-Benzin

petrol pump-Benzinpumpe

petrol station-Tankstelle

unleaded-Bleifrei-Benzin

bike-Fahrrad

camper van-Wohnmobil

bus-Bus

car-Auto

caravan-Wohnwagen

coach-Reisebus

lorry-Lastwagen

minibus-Minibus

moped-Moped

motorbike-Motorrad (informell)

scooter-Motorroller

taxi-Taxi

tractor-Traktor

truck-Lastwagen (amerikanisches Englisch)

van-Van

car hire-Autoverleih

car keys-Autoschlüssel

cyclist-Fahrradfahrer

driver-Fahrer, Fahrerin

garage-Werkstatt

mechanic-Mechaniker, Mechanikerin

insurance-Versicherung

passenger-Beifahrer

pedestrian-Fußgänger

reverse gear-Rückwärtsgang

road map-Straßenkarte

second-hand-gebraucht

speed-Geschwindigkeit

traffic-Verkehr

tyre pressure-Reifendruck

vehicle-Fahrzeug

to accelerate-beschleunigen

to brake-bremsen

to change gear-schalten

to drive-fahren

to overtake-überholen

to reverse-rückwärts fahren

to slow down-abbremsen

to speed up-beschleunigen

to steer-lenken

accelerator-Gaspedal

brake pedal-Bremse

clutch pedal-Kupplung

fuel gauge-Tankanzeige

gear stick-Schaltknüppel

handbrake-Handbremse

speedometer-Tachometer

steering wheel-Lenkrad

temperature gauge-Temperaturanzeige

warning light-Warnlicht

Mechanische Teile

battery-Batterie

brakes-Bremsen

clutch-Kupplung

engine-Motor

fan belt-Keilriemen

exhaust-Auspuff

exhaust pipe-Auspuffrohr

gear box-Getriebe

ignition-Zündung

radiator-Kühler

spark plug-Zündkerze

windscreen wiper-Scheibenwischer

air conditioning-Klimaanlage

automatic-Automatik

central locking-Zentralverriegelung

manual-Handschaltung

tax disc-Steuerplakette

sat nav-Satellitennavigation

brake light-Bremslicht

hazard lights-Warnblinker

headlamp-Scheinwerfer

indicators-Blinker

rear view mirror-Rückspiegel

sidelights-Standlicht

wing mirror-Seitenspiegel

Andere Teile

aerial-Antenne

back seat-Rücksitz

bonnet-Motorhaube

boot-Kofferraum

bumper-Stoßstange

child seat-Kindersitz

cigarette lighter-Zigarettenanzünder

dashboard-Armaturenbrett

front seat-Vordersitz

fuel tank-Kraftstofftank

glove compartment-Handschuhfach

glovebox-Handschuhfach

heater-Heizung

number plate-Kennzeichen

passenger seat-Beifahrersitz

petrol tank-Benzintank

roof-Dach

roof rack-Dachgepäckträger

seatbelt-Anschnallgurt

spare wheel-Ersatzreifen

tow bar-Abschleppstange

tyre-Reifen

wheel-Rad

window-Fenster

windscreen-Windschutzscheibe

Chapter 11 – Authorities

If you have to deal with authorities, it's good to know some of the phrases to explain yourself and get out of a difficult situation.

Ich habe nichts falsch gemacht. >> I haven't done anything wrong.

Es war ein Missverständniss. >> It was a misunderstanding.

Wohin bringen Sie mich? >> Where are you taking me?

Nehmen Sie mich fest? >> Am I under arrest?

Ich bin ein amerikansicher/australischer/britscher/kanadischer Staatsangehöriger. >> I am an American/Australian/British/Canadian citizen.

Ich bin ein deutscher/österreichischer/schweizer Staatsangehöriger. >> I am a German/Austrian/Swiss citizen.

Ich will mit der amerikanischen/australischen/britischen/kanadischen Botschaft/Konsulat sprechen. >> I need to talk to the American/Australian/British/Canadian embassy/consulate.

Ich möchte mit einem Anwalt sprechen. >> I want to talk to a lawyer.

Kann ich nicht einfach eine Buße bezahlen? >> Can't I just pay a fine now?

Chapter 12 – Emergencies

In case of an emergency, make sure to use these phrases:

Hilfe! - Help!

Feuer! - Fire!

Bitte gehen Sie! – Please go away!

Ich rufe die Polizei. - I'll call the police.

Es ist dringend! - It's urgent!

Ich bin vom Weg abgekommen. - I'm lost.

Ich habe ... - I've lost…

meinen Reisepaß verloren. - my passport.

meinen Autoschlüssel verloren. - my car keys.

Ich bin ausgeraubt worden. - I've been robbed.

Ich hatte einen Unfall. - I've had an accident.

Mein Auto hatte eine Panne. - My car has broken down.

Mein Auto ist gestohlen worden. - My car has been stolen.

Der Kühler wurde zu heiß. – The radiator has overheated.

Der Reifen ist geplatzt. - The tire has a puncture.

Die Batterie ist leer. - The battery is flat.

Die Kupplung ist defekt. - The clutch is broken.

Die Bremsen funktionieren nicht. - The brakes are not working.

Ich weiß nicht, woran es liegt. - I don't know what the problem is.

Ich brauche ... - I need…

Benzin. - Some petrol..

einen Mechaniker. - A mechanic.

die Polizei. - The police

Health

Ich brauche ... - I need…

einen Arzt. - a doctor.

ein Telefon. - A telephone.

einen Krankenwagen. - An ambulance.

einen Dolmetscher. - An interpreter.

Wo ist das Krankenhaus? - Where is the hospital?

Ich bin allergisch gegen Penizillin. - I'm allergic to penicillin.

Ich bin ... - I'm…

Diabetiker. - diabetic.

Asthmatiker. - asthmatic.

Ich brauche ... - I need…

einen Optiker. - An optician.

einen Zahnarzt. - A dentist.

Hier habe ich Schmerzen. - It hurts here.

Ich glaube, er/sie/es ist gebrochen. - I think it's broken.

At the pharmacy

Ich hätte gern … - I'd like some …

Zahnpasta - toothpaste

Paracetamol - paracetamol

Ich habe ein Rezept - I've got a prescription here from the doctor.

Haben Sie etwas gegen …? - have you got anything for …?

Herpesbläschen - cold sores

Halsschmerzen - a sore throat

rissige Lippen - chapped lips

Husten - a cough

Reiseübelkeit - travel sickness

Fußpilz - athlete's foot

Können Sie etwas gegen eine Erkältung empfehlen? - Can you recommend anything for a cold?

Ich habe … - I'm suffering from …

Heuschnupfen - hay fever

Verdauungsstörungen - indigestion

Durchfall - diarrhoea

Ich habe Ausschlag - I've got a rash.

Sie können diese Salbe ausprobieren - You could try this cream.

Wenn es nach einer Woche nicht weg ist, sollten Sie zum Arzt gehen - If it doesn't clear up after a week, you should see your doctor.

Haben Sie etwas, dass mir dabei hilft, mit dem Rauchen aufzuhören? - Have you got anything to help me stop smoking?

Haben Sie schon einmal Nikotinpflaster ausprobiert? - Have you tried nicotine patches?

Kann ich das hier rezeptfrei bekommen? - Can I buy this without a prescription?

Das gibt es nur auf Rezept - It's only available on prescription.

Hat es irgendwelche Nebenwirkungen? - Does it have any side-effects?

Es kann Sie schläfrig machen - It can make you feel drowsy.

Sie sollten keinen Alkohol trinken - You should avoid alcohol.

Kann ich bitte mit dem Apotheker sprechen? - I'd like to speak to the pharmacist, please.

Visiting a doctor

Ich möchte einen Doktor/Arzt sehen - I'd like to see a doctor.

Haben Sie einen Termin? - Do you have an appointment?

Ist es dringend? - Is it urgent?

Ich hätte gern einen Termin bei Dr. … - I'd like to make an appointment to see Dr …

Gibt es hier einen Arzt der … spricht? - Do you have any doctors who speak …?

Englisch - English

Sind Sie privat versichert? - Do you have private medical insurance?

Haben Sie eine Europäische Krankenversicherungkarte? - Have you got a European Health Insurance card?

Bitte nehmen Sie Platz - Please take a seat.

Der Arzt kann Sie jetzt sehen - The doctor's ready to see you now.

Was kann ich für Sie tun? - How can I help you?

Worin besteht Ihr Problem? - What's the problem?

Was für Symptome haben Sie? - What are your symptoms?

Ich habe ... - I've got a ...

Fieber - temperature

Halsschmerzen - sore throat

Kopfschmerzen - headache

Ausschlag - rash

Ich fühle mich seit einer Weile nicht wohl - I've been feeling sick.

Ich habe seit einer Weile Kopfschmerzen - I've been having headaches.

Meine Nase ist verstopft - I'm very congested.

Ich habe Gelenkschmerzen - My joints are aching.

Ich habe Durchfall - I've got diarrhea.

Ich habe Verstopfung - I'm constipated.

Ich habe eine Beule - I've got a lump/bump.

Ich habe einen geschwollenen ... - I've got a swollen ...

Knöchel - ankle

Ich habe starke Schmerzen - I'm in a lot of pain.

Ich habe ... - I've got a pain in my ...

Rückenschmerzen – back pain

Schmerzen in meiner Brust – chest pain

Ich glaube, ich habe mir einen Muskel in meinem Bein gezerrt - I think I've pulled a muscle in my leg.

Ich brauche … - I need …

neues Asthmaspray - another inhaler

etwas mehr Insulin - some more insulin

Ich habe Schwierigkeiten beim Atmen - I'm having difficulty breathing.

Ich fühle mich sehr schwach - I've got very little energy.

Ich bin seit einer Weile sehr müde - I've been feeling very tired.

Ich fühle mich seit einer Weile deprimiert - I've been feeling depressed.

Ich habe seit einer Weile Schlafstörungen - I've been having difficulty sleeping.

Wie lange fühlen Sie sich schon so? - How long have you been feeling like this?

Wie fühlen Sie sich im Allgemeinen? - How have you been feeling generally?

Besteht die Möglichkeit einer Schwangerschaft? - Is there any possibility you might be pregnant?

Ich bin möglicherweise schwanger - I think I might be pregnant.

Haben Sie irgendwelche Allergien? - Do you have any allergies?

Ich bin gegen Antibiotika allergisch - I'm allergic to antibiotics.

Nehmen Sie irgendwelche Medikamente? - Are you on any sort of medication?

Ich brauche eine Krankschreibung - I need a sick note.

Darf ich mir das mal ansehen? - Can I have a look?

Wo tut es weh? - Where does it hurt?

Es tut hier weh - It hurts here.

Tut es weh, wenn ich hier Druck ausübe? - Does it hurt when I press here?

Ich werde … messen - I'm going to take your …

Ihren Blutdruck - blood pressure

Ihre Temperatur - temperature

Ihren Puls - pulse

Können Sie bitte Ihren Ärmel hochkrempeln? - Could you roll up your sleeve?

Ihr Blutdruck ist … - Your blood pressure's …

ziemlich niedrig - quite low

normal - normal

ziemlich hoch - rather high

sehr hoch - very high

Ihre Temperatur ist ... - Your temperature's ...

normal - normal

leicht erhöht - a little high

sehr hoch - very high

Machen Sie bitte den Mund auf - Open your mouth, please.

Bitte husten Sie - Cough, please.

Sie werden ein paar Stiche brauchen - You're going to need a few stiches.

Ich werde Ihnen eine Spritze geben - I'm going to give you an injection.

Wir müssen eine ... nehmen - We need to take a ...

Urinprobe - urine sample

Blutprobe - blood sample

Sie müssen eine Blutuntersuchung machen lassen - You need to have a blood test.

Ich werde Ihnen Antibiotika verschreiben - I'm going to prescribe you some antibiotics.

Nehmen Sie davon dreimal täglich zwei - Take two of these pills three times a day.

Gehen Sie mit diesem Rezept zur Apotheke - Take this prescription to the chemist.

Rauchen Sie? - Do you smoke?

Sie sollten mit dem Rauchen aufhören - You should stop smoking.

Wieviel Alkohol trinken Sie pro Woche - How much alcohol do you drink a week?

Sie sollten das Trinken einschränken - You should cut down on your drinking.

Sie sollten versuchen, Ihr Gewicht zu reduzieren - You need to try and lose some weight.

Ich möchte Sie gern zum Röntgen schicken - I want to send you for an x-ray.

Ich möchte, dass Sie einen Spezialisten aufsuchen - I want you to see a specialist.

Important terms

aftershave - Aftershave

comb - Kamm

conditioner - Haarspülung

dental floss-Zahnseide

deodorant-Deodorant

hairbrush-Haarbürste

mouthwash-Mundspülung

nail file-Nagelfeile

nail scissors-Nagelschere

panty liners-Slipeinlage

perfume-Parfüm

razor-Rasierer

razorblade-Rasierklinge

sanitary towels-Damenbinden

shaving brush-Rasierpinsel

shaving cream-Rasiercreme

shaving foam-Rasierschaum

shaving gel-Rasiergel

shampoo-Shampoo

shower gel-Duschgel

soap-Seife

tampons-Tampons

toothbrush-Zahnbürste

toothpaste-Zahncreme

tweezers-Pinzette

cotton wool-Watte

eyeliner-Eyeliner

eyeshadow-Lidschatten

face powder-Gesichtspuder

foundation-Grundierung, Foundation

hair colouring or hair dye-Haarfarbe, Haartönung

hair gel-Haargel

hair spray-Haarspray

hair wax-Haarwachs

hand cream-Handcreme

lip gloss-Lipgloss

lipstick-Lippenstift

make-up-Makeup

mascara-Wimperntusche

moisturising cream-Feuchtigkeitscreme

nail varnish-Nagellack

nail varnish remover-Nagelackentferner

antiseptic-Antiseptikum

aspirin-Aspirin

athlete's foot powder-Fußpilzpuder

bandages-Bandagen

cough mixture-Hustensaft

diarrhoea tablets-Durchfalltabletten

emergency contraception - die Pille danach

eye drops-Augentropfen

first aid kit-Erste-Hilfe-Ausrüstung

hay fever tablets-Tabletten gegen Heuschnupfen

indigestion tablets-Tabletten gegen Magenverstimmungen

laxatives-Abführmittel

lip balm oder lip salve-Lippenbalsam

medicine-Medizin

nicotine patches-Nikotinpflaster

painkillers-Schmerzmittel

paracetamol-Paracetamol

plasters-Pflaster

pregnancy testing kit-Schwangerschaftstest

prescription-Rezept, Verschreibung

sleeping tablets-Schlaftabletten

thermometer-Thermometer

throat lozenges-Hustenpastille

tissues-Taschentücher

travel sickness tablets-Tabletten gegen Reisekrankheit

vitamin pills-Vitamintabletten

baby foods-Babynahrung

baby wipes-Babytücher

condoms-Kondome

contact lens solution-Kontaktlinsenlösung

disposable nappies-Wegwerfwindeln

hot water bottle-Wärmflasche

safety pins-Sicherheitsnadel

sun cream-Sonnencreme

sun block-Sonnenblocker, Sun-Blocker

beard-Bart

cheek-Wange

chin-Kinn

head-Kopf

hair-Haar

ear-Ohr

eye-Auge

eyebrow-Augenbraue

eardrum-Trommelfell

earlobe-Ohrläppchen

eyelash-Wimper

eyelid-Augenlid

forehead-Stirn

freckles-Sommersprossen

jaw-Kiefer

lip-Lippe

mouth-Mund

nose-Nase

nostril-Nasenloch

moustache-Schnurrbart

tongue-Zunge

tooth (Plural: teeth)-Zahn

wrinkles-Falten

Adam's apple-Adamsapfel

arm-Arm

armpit-Achsel

back-Rücken

breast-Brust, Busen

chest-Brust, Brustkorb

elbow-Ellbogen

hand-Hand

finger-Finger

fingernail-Fingernagel

forearm-Unterarm

knuckle-Knöchel

navel or belly button-Bauchnabel

neck-Hals

nipple-Nippel

palm-Handfläche

shoulder-Schulter

throat-Rachen

thumb-Daumen

waist-Taille

wrist-Handgelenk

ankle-Fußgelenk

anus-Anus

belly-Bauch

big toe-große Zeh

bottom-Po

buttocks-Gesäß

calf-Wade

foot (Plural: feet)-Fuß

genitals-Genitalien

groin-Leiste

heel-Ferse

hip-Hüfte

knee-Knie

leg-Bein

penis-Penis

pubic hair-Schamhaar

shin-Schiene

sole-Sohle

testicles-Hoden

thigh-Oberschenkel

toe-Zeh

toenail-Zehnagel

vagina-Vagina

cornea-Augenhornhaut

eye socket-Augenhöhle

eyeball-Augapfel

iris-Iris

retina-Retina

pupil-Pupille

Achilles tendon-Achillessehne

artery-Arterie

appendix-Blinddarm

bladder-Blase

blood vessel-Blutgefäß

brain-Gehirn

cartilage-Knorpel

colon-Darm

gall bladder oder gallbladder-Galle

heart-Herz

intestines-Eingeweide

large intestine-Dickdarm

small intestine-Dünndarm

kidneys-Nieren

ligament-Band

liver-Leber

lungs-Lunge

oesophagus-Speiseröhre

pancreas-Bauchspeicheldrüse

organ-Organ

prostate gland oder prostate-Prostata

rectum-Enddarm

spleen-Milz

stomach-Bauch, Magen

tendon-Sehne

tonsils-Mandeln

vein-Vene

windpipe-Luftröhre

womb oder uterus-Gebärmutter

collarbone oder clavicle-Schlüsselbein

thigh bone oder femur-Oberschenkelknochen

humerus-Oberarmknochen

kneecap-Kniescheibe

pelvis-Becken

rib-Rippe

rib cage-Brustkorb

skeleton-Skelett

skull-Schädel

spine oder backbone-Wirbelsäule

vertebra (Plural: vertebrae)-Wirbel

Körperflüssigkeiten

bile-Galle

blood-Blut

mucus-Schleim

phlegm-Phlegma

saliva oder spit-Speichel

semen-Samen

sweat oder perspiration-Schweiß

tears-Tränen

urine-Urin

vomit-Erbrochenes

Andere verwandte Wörter

bone-Knoche

fat-Fett

flesh-Fleisch

gland-Drüse

joint-Gelenk

limb-Extremität

muscle-Muskel

nerve-Nerv

skin-Haut

digestive system-Verdauungstrakt

nervous system-Nervensystem

to breathe-atmen

to cry-weinen

to hiccup-aufstoßen

to have the hiccups-Schluckauf haben

to sneeze-nießen

to sweat oder to perspire-schwitzen

to urinate-urinieren

to vomit-erbrechen/speiben

to yawn-gähnen

smell-Geruchssinn

touch-Tastsinn

sight-Sehen

hearing-Gehör

taste-Geschmackssinn

to smell-riechen

to touch-anfassen

to see-sehen

to hear-hören

to taste-schmecken

Chapter 13 - Services and repairs

If you have personal items that require repair or cleaning, these phrases will be helpful.

Können Sie mir sagen, wo ich ... zur Reparatur bringen kann? - Do you know where I can get my ... repaired?

Telefon/Handy – phone/mobile phone

meine Uhr - my watch

mein Fotoapparat - camera

meine Schuhe - shoes

Der Bildschirm ist kaputt - The screen's broken.

Mit ... stimmt was nicht - There's something wrong with ...

meiner Uhr - my watch

diesem Radio - this radio

Reparieren Sie ...? - Do you do ... repairs?

Fernseher - television

Computer - computer

Laptops - laptop

Was wird es ungefähr kosten? - How much will it cost?

Wann wird es fertig sein? - When will it be ready?

Wie lange wird es dauern? - How long will it take?

Ich kann es jetzt gleich erledigen - I can do it straight away

... ist es fertig - it'll be ready ...

bis morgen - by tomorrow

bis nächste Woche - next week

Innerhalb der nächsten zwei Wochen werde ich es nicht schaffen - I won't be able to do it for at least two weeks.

Können Sie es reparieren? - Are you able to repair it?

Wir können es nicht selbst machen - We can't do it here.

Wir müssen es zurück zum Hersteller schicken - We're going to have to send it back to the manufacturers.

Eine Reparatur lohnt sich nicht - It's not worth repairing.

Meine Uhr ist stehengeblieben - My watch has stopped.

Darf ich mal sehen? - Can I have a look at it?

Ich glaube, sie braucht eine neue Batterie - I think it needs a new battery.

Ich wollte … abholen - I've come to collect my …

meine Uhr - watch

meinen Computer - computer

Photography

Könnten Sie die Fotos auf dieser Speicherkarte für mich drucken? - Could you print the photos on this memory card for me?

Könnten Sie die Fotos auf diesem Memorystick für mich drucken? - Could you print the photos on this memory stick for me?

Möchten Sie die Bilder in Matt oder Hochglanz? - Would you like matte or gloss prints?

Welche Größe sollen die Bilder haben? - What size prints would you like?

Post office

Wie viel kostet eine Briefmarke für einen Eilbrief? - How much is a first class stamp?

Wie viel kostet eine Briefmarke für eine normale Sendung? - How much is a second class stamp?

Ich hätte gern …, bitte - I'd like …, please

Einen Briefumschlag - an envelope

ein Paket Briefumschläge - a packet of envelopes

einen gepolsterten Briefumschlag - a jiffy bag

Könnte ich bitte ... haben? - Could I have ..., please?

eine Briefmarke für einen Eilbrief? - a first class stamp

eine Briefmarke für eine normale Sendung? - a second class stamp

ein Briefmarkenheft für Eilbriefe - a book of first class stamps

einige Briefmarken für Eilbriefe - some first class stamps

Wie viele hätten Sie gerne? - How many would you like?

Wie viele sind in einem Heft? - How many are there in a book?

Ich möchte das hier nach ... schicken - I'd like to send this to ...

Ich möchte dieses Paket nach ... schicken - I'd like to send this parcel to ...

Wieviel kostet dieser Brief nach/in die ...? - How much will it cost to send this letter to ...?

Würden Sie es bitte auf die Waage legen? - Can you put it on the scales, please?

Ich würde diesen Brief gerne per ... verschicken - I'd like to send this letter by ...

Einschreiben - Recorded Delivery

Eilbrief mit Versicherung - Special Delivery

Wo ist der Briefkasten? - Where's the postbox?

Wann muss ich das hier spätestens nach / in die ... abschicken, damit es rechtzeitig zu Weihnachten ankommt? - What's the last date I can post this to ... to arrive in time for Christmas?

Ich würde gerne ein Paket abholen - I've come to collect a parcel.

Ich würde gerne diese Rechnung bezahlen - I'd like to pay this bill.

Ich möchte gern Geld nach ... transferieren - I'd like to send some money to ...

Verkaufen Sie ...? - Do you sell ...?

Postkarten - postcards

Geburtstagskarten - birthday cards

Weihnachtskarten - Christmas cards

Ich möchte gern meinen Fernseher anmelden - I'd like to get a TV licence.

Ich möchte gern meine Fernsehlizenz verlängern - I need to renew my TV licence.

Würden Sie bitte dieses Formular ausfüllen? - Can you fill in this form, please?

Haben Sie ...? - Do you have a ...?

einen Fotoautomaten - photo booth

einen Fotokopierer - photocopier

Bank

Ich möchte gern einhundert Euro abheben, bitte - I'd like to withdraw €100, please.

Ich möchte gern Geld abheben - I want to make a withdrawal.

Wie hätten Sie es gern? - How would you like the money?

in Zehnern, bitte - in tens, please

Könnten Sie mir ein paar kleinere Scheine geben? - Could you give me some smaller notes?

Ich wüder das gerne einzahlen, bitte - I'd like to pay this in, please.

Ich möchte gern diesen Scheck einlösen, bitte - I'd like to pay this check in, please.

Wie lange dauert es bis der Scheck eingelöst ist? - How many days will it take for the check to clear?

Haben Sie ...? - Have you got any ...?

einen Ausweis dabei - identification

Ich habe ... - I've got my ...

meinen Pass dabei - passport

meinen Führerschein dabei - driving licence

meinen Personalausweis dabei - ID card

Ihr Konto ist überzogen - Your account's overdrawn.

Ich würde gerne Geld auf dieses Konto überweisen - I'd like to transfer some money to this account.

Könnten Sie bitte tausend Euro von meinem Girokonto auf mein Sparkonto überweisen? - Could you transfer €1000 from my current account to my deposit account?

Ich möchte ein Bankkonto eröffnen - I'd like to open an account.

Ich möchte ein Privatkonto eröffnen - I'd like to open a personal account.

Ich möchte ein Geschäftskonto eröffnen - I'd like to open a business account.

Können Sie mir bitte meinen Kontostand sagen? - Could you tell me my balance, please?

Könnte ich bitte einen Kontoauszug haben? - Could I have a statement, please?

Ich möchte gern etwas Geld wechseln - I'd like to change some money.

Ich möchte gern Fremdwährung bestellen - I'd like to order some foreign currency.

wie lautet der Wechselkurs für Euro? - What's the exchange rate for euros?

Ich hätte gern ... - I'd like some ...

Euro - euros

US-Dollar - US dollars

Kann ich bitte ein neues Scheckbuch haben? - Could I order a new checkbook, please?

Ich möchte einen Scheck zurückziehen - I'd like to cancel a check.

Ich möchte diesen Dauerauftrag beenden - I'd like to cancel this standing order.

Wo ist der nächste Geldautomat/Bankomat? - Where's the nearest cash machine?

Wie hoch ist der Zinssatz für dieses Konto? - What's the interest rate on this account?

Wie hoch ist der aktuelle Zinssatz für Privatkredite? - What's the current interest rate for personal loans?

Ich habe meine Bankkarte verloren - I've lost my bank card.

Ich möchte eine ... melden - I want to report a ...

verlorene Kreditkarte - lost credit card

gestohlene Kreditkarte - stolen credit card

Wir haben ein gemeinsames Konto - We've got a joint account.

Ich möchte gern eine Adressänderung melden - I'd like to tell you about a change of address.

Ich habe das Passwort für mein Online-Konto vergessen - I've forgotten my Internet banking password.

Ich habe die PIN für meine Karte vergessen - I've forgotten the PIN number for my card.

Ich werde Ihnen ein neues senden - I'll have a new one sent out to you.

Ich hätte gern einen Termin mit ... - Could I make an appointment to see ...?

dem Geschäftsführer - the manager

einem Finanzberater - a financial advisor

Ich hätte gern eine Beratung zum Thema Hypothek - I'd like to speak to someone about a mortgage.

ATM

Führen Sie ihre Karte ein - Insert your card.

Geben Sie ihre PIN ein - Enter your PIN.

Falsche PIN - Incorrect PIN

Eingabe - Enter

Korrektur - Correct

Abbruch - Cancel

Bargeld abheben - Withdraw cash

Anderer Betrag - Other amount

Bitte warten - Please wait

Ihr Geld wird gezählt - Your cash is being counted.

Kontostand nicht ausreichend - Insufficient funds

Kontostand - Balance

Auf dem Bildschirm - On screen

Ausgedruckt - Printed

Weiterer Dienst? - Another service?

Wollen Sie eine Rechnung haben? - Would you like a receipt?

Karte entnehmen - Remove card.

Verlassen - Quit

Important terms

laptop-Laptop

desktop computer-Computer

tablet computer-Tablet

PC-PC

screen-Bildschirm

keyboard-Tastatur

mouse-Maus

monitor-Bildschirm

printer-Drucker

wireless router-WLAN Router

cable-Kabel

hard drive-Festplatte

speakers-Lautsprecher

power cable-Stromkabel

email-E-Mail

to email-e-mailen

to send an email-eine E-Mail senden

email address-E-Mailadresse

username-Benutzername

password-Passwort

to reply-antworten

to forward-weiterleiten

new message-neue Nachricht

attachment-Anhang

to plug in-einstecken

to unplug-ausstöpseln

to switch on or to turn on-anmachen

to switch off or to turn off-ausmachen

to start up-hochfahren

to shut down-herunterfahren

to restart-erneut einschalten

the Internet-das Internet

website-Webseite

broadband internet or broadband-Breitband-Internet

ISP-Internetdienstanbieter

firewall-Firewall

web hosting-Webhosting

wireless internet or WiFi-drahtloses Netz oder WLAN

to download-herunterladen

to browse the Internet-im Internet suchen

Andere nützliche Wörter

file-Datei

folder-Verzeichnis

document-Dokument

hardware-Hardware

software-Software

network-Netzwerk

to scroll up-nach oben scrollen

to scroll down-nach unten scrollen

to log on-einloggen

to log off-ausloggen

space bar-Leertaste

virus-Virus

antivirus software-Antiviren-Software

processor speed-Prozessorgeschwindigkeit

memory-Speicher

word processor-Textverarbeitungsprogramm

database-Datenbank

spreadsheet-Kalkulationstabelle

to print-drucken

to type-tippen

lower case letter-Kleinbuchstaben

upper case letter oder capital letter-Großbuchstaben

Chapter 14 – Spare Time

When you have spare time, you'll probably visit the theater, museum or club. Whatever the case is, these phrases may help you:

Teathre

Läuft ... etwas in Theater? - Is there anything on at the theatre ...?

heute Abend - tonight

diese Woche - this week

diesen Monat - this month

Wie lange läuft das Stück noch? - When's the play on until?

Wer spielt darin mit? - Who's in it?

Was für ein Stück ist es? - What type of production is it?

Es ist ... - It's ...

eine Komödie - a comedy

eine Tragödie - a tragedy

ein Musical - a musical

eine Oper - an opera

ein Ballet - a ballet

Hast du das Stück schon mal gesehen? - Have you seen it before?

Um wieviel Uhr beginnt die Vorstellung? - What time does the performance start?

Wann ist es zuende? - What time does it finish?

Wo ist die Garderobe? - Where's the cloakroom?

Möchten Sie gern ein Programmheft? - Would you like a program?

Kann ich bitte ein Programmheft haben? - Could I have a program, please?

Sollen wir für die Pause etwas zu trinken bestellen? - Shall we order some drinks for the interval?

Wir sollten zu unseren Plätzen zurückgehen - We'd better go back to our seats.

Hat es dir gefallen? - Did you enjoy it?

The club

Hast du Lust, heute abend in die Disco zu gehen? - Do you want to go to a club tonight?

Kennst du eine gute Disco hier in der Nähe? - Do you know any good clubs near here?

Bis wann haben Sie geöffnet? - What time are you open until?

Wann schließen Sie? - What time do you close?

Was kostet der Eintritt? - How much is it to get in?

Gibt es eine Kleiderordnung? - Is there a dress code?

An welchen Abenden haben Sie geöffnet? - What nights are you open?

Was für eine Art Musik spielen Sie? - What sort of music is it?

Was gibt es heute Abend? - What's on tonight?

Gibt es heute Abend Livemusik bei Ihnen? - Do you have any live music tonight?

Sorry, Sie können nicht rein - Sorry, you can't come in.

Sie können nicht mit Turnschuhen rein - You can't come in with trainers on.

Heute Nacht ist eine Privatparty - There's a private party tonight.

Der Klub ist voll - The club's full.

Ich bin auf der Gästeliste - I'm on the guest list.

Ich bin ein Mitglied - I'm a member.

Wo ist die Garderobe? - Where's the cloakroom?

Wie gefällt dir der DJ? - What do you think of the DJ?

Die Musik ist super - The music's great!

Es ist viel los heute Abend - It's very lively tonight.

Es ist ein bisschen leer - It's a bit empty.

Ziemlich tote Hose hier (Slang) - It's dead in here.

Wo ist die Bar? - Where's the bar?

An der Bar ist eine lange Schlange - There's a long queue at the bar.

Es ist zu laut - It's too loud.

Es ist zu heiss hier drinnen - It's too hot in here.

Möchtest du nach Hause gehen? - Are you ready to go home?

Ich gehe nach Hause - I'm going home.

Flirting – Small Talk

Kann ich mich setzen? - May I join you?

Darf ich Dir ein Getränk ausgeben? - May I buy you something to drink?

Bist Du oft hier? - Do you come here often?

Und, was machst du beruflich? - So, what do you do for a living?

Willst Du tanzen? - Do you want to dance?

Möchtest du kurz rausgehen? - Would you like to get some fresh air?

Willst Du auf eine andere Party gehen? - Do you want to go to a different party?

Lass uns losgehen! - Let's get out of here!

Zu mir oder zu dir? - My place or yours?

Möchtest Du bei mir einen Film schauen? - Would you like to watch a movie at my place?

Hast Du heute Abend etwas vor? - Do you have any plans for tonight?

Würdest Du mit mir mal Mittagessen/Abendessen gehen? - Would you like to have lunch/dinner with me sometime?

Würdest Du mit mir einen Kaffee trinken gehen? - Would you like to go get a coffee?

Kann ich Dich nach Hause begleiten/fahren? - May I walk/drive you home?

Würdest Du Dich gern noch einmal treffen? - Would you like to meet again?

Danke für den schönen Abend. Gute Nacht! - Thank you for a lovely evening!

Möchtest Du auf einen Kaffee hereinkommen? - Would you like to come inside for a coffee?

Du siehst hinreißend aus! - You're gorgeous!

Du bist lustig! - You're funny!

Du hast wunderschöne Augen! - You have beautiful eyes!

Du bist eine gute Tänzerin/ein guter Tänzer! - You're a great dancer!

Du siehst wunderschön in dem Kleid/T-Shirt/Hemd aus! - You look beautiful in that dress/shirt!

Ich habe den ganzen Tag an Dich gedacht! - I have been thinking about you all day!

Es war schön, mit Dir zu reden! - It's been really nice talking to you!

Ich habe kein Interesse. - I'm not interested.

Lass mich in Ruhe. - Leave me alone.

Verschwinde/Hau ab! - Get lost!

Fass mich nicht an! - Don't touch me!

Nimm deine Finger weg! - Get your hands off me!

Museum and Gallery

Was kostet der Eintritt? - How much is it to get in?

Kostet es Eintritt? - Is there an admission charge?

Nur für die Ausstellung - Only for the exhibition.

Wann schließen Sie? - What time do you close?

Das Museum ist montags geschlossen - The museum's closed on Mondays.

Darf ich fotografieren? - Can I take photographs?

Möchten Sie einen Audio-Guide? - Would you like an audio-guide?

Gibt es heute geführte Touren? - Are there any guided tours today?

Wann beginnt die nächste geführte Tour? - What time does the next guided tour start?

Wo ist die Garderobe? - Where's the cloakroom?

Wir müssen unsere Taschen an der Garderobe abgeben - We have to leave our bags in the cloakroom.

Haben Sie einen Übersichtsplan des Museums? - Do you have a plan of the museum?

Wer hat dieses Bild gemalt? - Who's this painting by?

Dieses Museum hat eine sehr gute Sammlung von … - This museum's got a very good collection of …

Ölgemälden - oil paintings

Aquarellen - watercolours

Porträts - portraits

Landschaftsbildern - landscapes

Skulpturen - sculptures

antiken Kunstgegenständen - ancient artifacts

Keramik - pottery

magst du …? - do you like …?

moderne Kunst - modern art

klassische Gemälde - classical paintings

impressionistische Gemälde - impressionist paintings

Important terms

avenue-Allee

bus shelter-Wartehäuschen

bus stop-Bushaltestelle

high street-Haupteinkaufsstraße

lamppost-Laternenpfahl

parking meter-Parkuhr

pavement-Bürgersteig

pedestrian crossing-Fußgängerüberweg

pedestrian subway-Fußgängerunterführung

side street-Seitenstraße

signpost-Hinweisschild

square-Platz

street-Straße

taxi rank-Taxistand

telephone box oder telephone booth-Telefonhäuschen

antique shop-Antiquitätenladen

bakery-Bäckerei

barbers-Frisörsalon für Männer

beauty salon-Schönheitssalon

betting shop or bookmakers-Wettbüro

bookshop-Buchhandlung

butchers-Metzgerei

car showroom-Autohändler

charity shop-Gebrauchtwarenladen, dessen Umsatz für wohltätige Zwecke bestimmt ist

chemists oder pharmacy-Apotheke

clothes shop-Bekleidungsgeschäft

delicatessen-Feinkostgeschäft

department store-Kaufhaus

DIY store-Baumarkt

dress shop-Bekleidungsgeschäft

dry cleaners-Trockenreinigung

electrical shop-Elektronikgeschäft

estate agents-Immobilienbüro

fishmongers-Fischhändler

florists-Blumenladen

garden centre-Gartenzentrum

general store-Gemischtwarenladen

gift shop-Geschenkartikelladen

greengrocers-Gemüsehändler

hairdressers-Frisörsalon

hardware shop-Eisenwarenladen

kiosk-Kiosk

launderette-Waschsalon

newsagents-Zeitschriftenladen

off licence-Wein- und Spirituosenhandlung

second-hand bookshop-Antiquariat

second-hand clothes shop-Second-Hand-Laden

shoe repair shop-Schuhreperatur

shoe shop-Schuhgeschäft

sports shop-Sportgeschäft

stationers-Schreibwarengeschäft

supermarket-Supermarkt

tailors-Schneider

tattoo parlor or tattoo studio-Tattooladen

toy shop-Spielzeugladen

apartment block-Wohnblock

art gallery-Kunstgalerie

bank-Bank

bar-Bar

block of flats-Mietshaus

building society-Wohnungsbaugesellschaft

café-Café

cathedral-Kathedrale

church-Kirche

cinema-Kino

concert hall-Konzerthalle

dentists-Zahnarzt

doctors--Arzt

fire station-Feuerwehr

fish and chip shop-Pommesbude

chestnuts and potatoes stand – Maronistand

garage-Garage; Autowerkstatt

gym-Fitnessstudio

health centre-Gesundheitszentrum

hospital-Krankenhaus

hotel-Hotel

internet cafe-Internet Café

leisure centre oder sports centre-Freizeitzentrum

library-Bücherei

mosque-Moschee

museum-Museum

office block-Bürogebäude

petrol station-Tankstelle

police station-Polizeiwache

post office-Postamt

pub-Kneipe

restaurant-Restaurant

school-Schule

shopping centre-Einkaufszentrum

skyscraper-Wolkenkratzer

swimming baths-Schwimmbad

synagogue-Synagoge

theatre-Theater

tower block-Hochhaus

town hall-Rathaus

university-Universität

vets-Tierarzt

wine bar-Weinbar

bowling alley-Bowlinghalle

bus station-Busbahnhof

car park-Parkplatz

cemetery-Friedhof

children's playground-Spielplatz

marketplace-Marktplatz

multi-storey car park-Parkhaus

park-Park

skate park-Skatepark

stadium-Stadion

town square-zentraler Platz

train station-Bahnhof

zoo-Zoo

Chapter 15 – Useful words and terms

Here are some useful words and their translation so you can quickly express your thoughts:

Landscape and geographical terms

countryside-Land

hill-Hügel

mountain-Berg

valley-Tal

wood-Wald

forest-Wald (große Fläche)

copse-Hain

field-Feld

meadow-Wiese

plain-Ebene

moor-Heide

bog-Moor

swamp-Sumpf

hedge-Hecke

path-Pfad

fence-Zaun

wall-Mauer

ditch-Graben

gate-Tor

farm-Bauernhof

bridge-Brücke

desert-Wüste

glacier-Gletscher

jungle-Dschungel

rainforest-Regenwald

volcano-Vulkan

stream-Bach

river-Fluss

canal-Kanal

pond-Teich

lake-See

reservoir-Reservoir

waterfall-Wasserfall

well-Brunnen

dam-Damm

power station-Elektrizitätswerk

wind farm-Windfarm

mine-Miene

quarry-Steinbruch

agriculture-Landwirtschaft

barn-Scheune

farmhouse-Bauernhaus

crop-Getreide

harvest-Ernte

hay-Heu

wheat-Weizen

irrigation-Bewässerung

livestock-Vieh

to plough-pflügen

to harvest-ernten

ocean-Ozean

sea-Meer

coast oder shore-Küste

beach-Strand

cliff-Kliff

island-Insel

peninsula-Halbinsel

rock-Fels

tide-Gezeiten

wave-Welle

pier-Pier

lighthouse-Leuchtturm

harbour-Hafen

oil rig-Ölbohrplattform

Other useful words-Andere nützliche Wörter

country-Land

city-Stadt (Großstadt)

town-Stadt

village-Dorf

eruption-Ausbruch

earthquake-Erdbeben

tsunami-Tsunami

avalanche-Lawine

landslide-Erdrutsch

lava-Lava

capital city oder capital-Hauptstadt

border-Grenze

national park-Nationalpark

North Pole-Nordpol

South Pole-Südpol

Equator-Äquator

longitude-Längengrad

latitude--Breitengrand

sea level-Meeresspiegel

erosion-Erosion

pollution-Verschmutzung

atmosphere-Atmosphäre

environment-Umwelt

population-Bevölkerung

famine-Hungersnot

fossil fuel-fossiler Brennstoff

energy-Energie

unemployment-Arbeitslosigkeit

landscape-Landschaft

literacy-Fähigkeit zu lesen

malnutrition-Unterernährung

migration-Völkerwanderung

radiation-Strahlung

nuclear energy-Atomenergie

crater-Krater

sand dune-Sanddüne

trade-Handel

urban-urban

rural-ländlich

economy-Wirtschaft

poverty-Armut

slum-Armutsviertel

life expectancy-Lebenserwartung

The weather

sun-Sonne

sunshine-Sonnenschein

rain-Regen

snow-Schnee

hail-Hagel

drizzle-Nieselregen

sleet-Schneeregen

shower-Regenschauer

mist-leichter Nebel

fog-dichter Nebel

cloud-Wolke

rainbow-Regenbogen

wind-Wind

breeze-Brise

strong winds-starker Wind

thunder-Donner

lightning-Blitz

storm-Sturm

thunderstorm-Gewitter

gale-starker Wind, Sturm

tornado-Tornado

hurricane-Hurrikan

flood-Flut, Überschwemmung

frost-Frost

ice-Eis

drought-Dürre

heat wave-Hitzewelle

windy-windig

cloudy-bewölkt

foggy-neblig (dicht)

misty-neblig (leicht)

icy-eisig

frosty-frostig

stormy-stürmisch

dry-trocken

wet-nass

hot-heiß

cold-kalt

chilly-kühl

sunny-sonnig

rainy-regnerisch, verregnet

fine-schön

dull-bedeckt

overcast-bewölkt

humid-feucht

raindrop-Regentropfen

snowflake-Schneeflocke

hailstone-Hagelkorn

to melt-schmelzen

to freeze-frieren

to thaw-tauen

to snow-schneien

to rain-regnen

to hail-hageln

weather forecast-Wettervorhersage

rainfall-Niederschlag

temperature-Temperatur

humidity-Luftfeuchtigkeit

thermometer-Thermometer

high pressure-Hochdruck

low pressure-Tiefdruck

barometer-Barometer

degree-Grad

Celsius--Celsius

Fahrenheit-Fahrenheit

Home appliance

battery-Batterie

candle-Kerze

cotton-Baumwolle

envelopes-Briefumschläge

firelighters-Feueranzünder

fuse-Sicherung

glue-Klebstoff

light bulb-Glühbirne

lighter-Feuerzeug

matches-Streichhölzer

needle-Nadel

safety pin-Sicherheitsnadel

scissors-Schere

sellotape-Klebestreifen, Tesafilm

stamps-Briefmarken

pen-Kugelschreiber

pencil-Bleistift

tissues-Taschentücher

toilet paper oder toilet roll-Toilettenpapier

toothpaste-Zahnpasta

tube of toothpaste-Zahnpastatube

writing paper-Schreibpapier

bin bag oder bin liner-Müllbeutel

bleach-Bleiche

detergent-Spülmittel

disinfectant-Desinfektionsmittel

dustbin bag-Müllsack

duster-Staublappen

fabric softener-Weichspüler

floorcloth-Putzlappen

furniture polish-Möbelpolitur

hoover bag-Staubsaugerbeutel

shoe polish-Schuhwichse

soap-Seife

washing powder-Waschpulver

Animals

dog-Hund

cat-Katze

rabbit- Kaninchen

hamster-Hamster

goldfish-Goldfisch

cow-Kuh

sheep (Plural: sheep)-Schaf

pig-Schwein

horse-Pferd

chicken-Hühnchen

fox-Fuchs

deer (Plural: deer)-Hirsch

mouse (Plural: mice)-Maus

rat-Ratte

frog-Frosch

snake-Schlange

lion-Löwe

tiger-Tiger

monkey-Affe

elephant-Elefant

giraffe-Giraffe

bear-Bär

pigeon-Taube

crow-Krähe

dove-Taube

owl-Eule

eagle-Adler

ant-Ameise

fly-Fliege

spider-Spinne

bee-Biene

wasp-Wespe

butterfly-Schmetterling

cod (Plural: cod)-Kabeljau

trout (Plural: trout)-Forelle

salmon (Plural: salmon)-Lachs

tuna (Plural: tuna)-Thunfisch

shark-Hai

crab-Krabbe

tail-Schwanz

fur-Fell

claw-Klaue

paw-Tatze

hoof-Huf

mane-Mähne

trunk-Rüssel

snout-Schnauze

Flowers

bracken-Farnkraut

brambles-Brombeerstrauch

bush-Busch

cactus (Plural: cacti)-Kaktus

corn-Mais

fern-Farn

flower-Blume

grass-Gras

heather-Heide

herb-Kraut

ivy-Efeu

moss-Moos

mushroom-Pilz (gewöhnlich essbar)

nettle-Nessel

shrub-Strauch

thistle-Distel

toadstool-Giftpilz

tree-Baum

weed-Unkraut

wheat-Weizen

wild flower-Wildblume

bluebell-Hasenglöckchen

buttercup-Butterblume

carnation-Nelke

chrysanthemum-Chrysantheme

crocus-Krokus

daffodil-Osterglocke

dahlia-Dahlie

daisy-Gänseblümchen

dandelion-Löwenzahn

forget-me-not-Vergissmeinnicht

foxglove-Fingerhut

geranium-Geranie

lily-Lilie

orchid-Orchidee

pansy-Stiefmütterchen

poppy-Mohn

primrose-Schlüsselblume

rose-Rose

snowdrop-Schneeglöckchen

sunflower-Sonnenblume

tulip-Tulpe

waterlily-Weiße Seerose

bouquet of flowers oder flower bouquet-Blumenstrauß

bunch of flowers-Blumenstrauß

berry-Beere

blossom-Blüte

bud-Knospe

flower-Blüte

leaf-Blatt

petal-Blütenblatt

pollen-Pollen

root-Wurzel

stalk-Stiel

stem-Stamm

thorn-Dorn

alder-Erle

ash-Esche

beech-Buche

birch-Birke

cedar-Zeder

elm-Ulme

fir-Tanne

hazel-Hasel

hawthorn-Weissdorn

holly-Stechpalme

lime-Linde

maple-Ahorn

oak-Eiche

plane-Platane

pine-Kiefer

poplar-Pappel

sycamore-Sycamore

weeping willow-Trauerweide

willow-Weide

yew-Eibe

apple tree-Apfelbaum

cherry tree-Kirschbaum

chestnut tree-Kastanienbaum

coconut tree-Kokonusspalme

fig tree-Feigenbaum

horse chestnut tree-Rosskastanie

olive tree-Olivenbaum

pear tree-Birnenbaum

plum tree-Pflaumenbaum

bark-Rinde

branch-Ast

pine cone-Kiefernzapfen

sap-Pflanzensaft

tree stump oder stump-Baumstumpf

trunk-Baumstamm

twig-Zweig

fruit tree-Obstbaum

palm tree-Palme

evergreen-immergrün

coniferous-zapfentragend

deciduous-laubabwerfend

Useful adjectives

big-groß

small oder little-klein

fast-schnell

slow-langsam

good-gut

bad-schlecht

expensive-teuer

cheap-billig

thick-dick

thin-dünn

narrow-eng

wide-breit

broad-breit

loud-laut

quiet-leise

intelligent-intelligent

stupid-dumm

wet-nass

dry-trocken

heavy-schwer

light-leicht

hard-hart

soft-weich

shallow-flach, seicht

deep-tief

easy-leicht

difficult-schwierig

weak-schwach

strong-stark

rich-reich

poor-arm

young-jung

old-alt

long-lang

short-kurz

high-hoch

low-tief

generous-großzügig

mean-geizig

true-richtig

false-falsch

beautiful-schön

ugly-hässlich

new-neu

old-alt

happy-fröhlich, glücklich

sad-traurig

safe-sicher

dangerous-gefährlich

early-früh

late-spät

light-hell

dark-dunkel

open-offen, geöffnet

closed oder shut-geschlossen, zu
tight- fest
loose-locker
full-voll
empty-leer
many-viele
few-wenige
alive-lebendig
dead-tot
hot-heiß
cold-kalt
interesting-interessant
boring-langweilig
lucky-glücklich
unlucky-unglücklich
important-wichtig
unimportant-unwichtig
right-richtig
wrong-falsch
far-weit
near-nahe
clean-sauber
dirty-schmutzig
nice-nett
nasty-gemein
pleasant-angenehm
unpleasant-unangenehm
excellent-ausgezeichnet

terrible-schrecklich

fair-fair

unfair-unfair

normal-normal

abnormal-anormal

Chapter 16 – Tips for learning a new language

Are you in the middle of planning your trip? Did you think of everything? First aid kit, papers & documents? Very good, but what about your foreign language skills? Have you ever thought how you'll express yourself? Unfortunately, many travelers neglect this topic and think that with English you can get anywhere. And some also assume that you can communicate well with your hands and feet. The question that you should ask yourself is:

What do I expect from my journey and which goal do I have?

To give you a little motivation, here are 5 advantages of being able to express yourself in the foreign language.

-You get to know the locals much more authentically.

-You understand the culture and attitude of people much better.

-You can negotiate more effectively.

-You do not waste valuable time, because you understand faster.

-You feel safer.

Just to keep it short: You do not have to learn the foreign language to perfection. But you should be able to communicate well. Here are some tips on how to learn certain basics quickly and effectively.

Are you ready? Okay, then we can start. Depending on how much time you have until the trip, you should use the time well. Which language level you achieve depends entirely on you. Here are some essential recommendations on how to learn a language.

1. Speak from the first day.

Unfortunately, many people follow a wrong approach when learning a language. A language is a means of communication and should therefore be lived rather than learned. There is no such thing as an "I am ready now." Therefore, just jump into the cold water and speak already at home from the first day on. That sounds horrible and silly? It does not matter, with time it will get better. It is best to set the goal not to miss a day when you have not used the foreign language in any form. Just try to implement everything you learn directly. So speak, write and think in your foreign language.

2. Immerse yourself in the foreign language at home.

This tip actually goes hand in hand with the first recommendation. To learn the foreign language quickly and efficiently, you have to integrate it firmly into your everyday life. It is not enough if you learn a few words from time to time and engage in grammar and pronunciation. This has to be done much more intensively. You have to dive properly into the foreign language. Just bring foreign countries to your home. By so-called "Immersion" you surround yourself almost constantly and everywhere with the learning language.

3.Change the language setting on devices.

For example, you could change the menu language of your smartphone or laptop from your native language to your learning language. Since you use your smartphone or your laptop every day, you know where to find something and learn some vocabulary along the way. Of course you can also do the same with your social networks like Facebook and Twitter. But watch out that you are always able to change back the menu language!

4.Use foreign language media.

You could, for example, get a foreign language newspaper. If that is not available or too expensive, then there are enough newspapers or news portals where you can read news online. Probably you are already familiar with the news through your native language, then the context is easier if you read the same messages again in the foreign language. Further aids are foreign-language films or series. It's probably best to start with a movie or series that you've already seen in your native language. The slang and common phrases can make it really hard for you. If you realize that you are not understanding it well, try the subtitle in the foreign language. If that does not work, then take the subtitle of your native language and try again. Even music should not be neglected in your foreign-language world. This has the advantage of teaching you a lot about the pronunciation and emphasis. Incidentally, you are getting a lot closer to the culture of the country.

5.Set notes in your apartment

If it does not bother you and others, spread little sticky notes with words in the apartment. Whether this is your toothbrush, the couch or the remote control, just place notes on as many objects and pieces of furniture as possible with the respective name of the object in the foreign language. As a result, you have the vocabulary all day long and memorize it automatically.

6.Learn the most important phrases

Another helpful tip is to think about what words and phrases you'll need before you travel. For example, you could write down how to reserve a hotel room or book a bus ride. Even how to order in the restaurant, ask someone for directions and how to communicate with the doctor or the police. Of course, this book is more than enough and you have all the phrases at one place.

7. Set clear goals

Last but not least, an important piece of advice: Set clear goals. Without goals, you will never get where you want to go. Since you have already booked your flight, you also have a deadline, to which you have reached a goal you have set. To accomplish this, you can now place mini orders. But stay realistic with your goals, especially in relation to your mini goals. If they are too big and not realistically achievable, you may lose your courage and give up. A good tip is also that you record your goals in writing because writing is like having a contract with yourself. It makes your goals more binding and makes you feel more obligated to stick to your schedule. The writing down also has the advantage that you have to formulate your goals more precisely and not forget them so quickly. Do not just try to formulate these goals, but really approach them and implement them.

Here are some examples of how you could define your goals:

Learn 300 words

Memorize 5 phrases

Write an email in the foreign language

Memorize important questions

Conduct a talk online via webcam

How can you achieve your goals?

Set Priorities: Be sure to rank your goals by importance!

Stay realistic: What is your current life situation?

Start today: Do not think about tomorrow or yesterday, but start today to reach your goals! The longer you wait, the less likely you are to achieve your goals.

Tell others about it: If others know about your goals, then you will do everything possible to reach them. Otherwise, you would have to admit defeat. This tip could of course make you stress, but will help you to work purposefully!

Change your habits: You may need to change something in your daily routine to achieve your goals. Do not hesitate and reject bad habits that get in your way!

Reward yourself: Every time you reach a partial goal, do something good! You know best what that can be!

Obviously, you do not have to punish yourself, but some people are more likely to do it than to be rewarded for success.

Let the imagination play: Imagine how it is when you reach your goals. What would you be capable of? What would you feel? This will motivate you immensely to work on your goals!

8. Humor

Do not feel sad, if it does not work right away. You may be embarrassing yourself in front of a native speaker because you mispronounce a word and make a completely different sense. Nobody will blame you. For most people it means a lot that you try to learn their language. And when they laugh then they do not mean that. But the most important thing is: have fun getting to know a new language! After all, you do not have any pressure, as you do at school.

Mastering the foreign language of your destination country has only advantages. You will learn to understand how people of a particular region think, what fears and worries they have and how they tackle life. You'll become more tolerant and see the world differently and, after your journey, you'll definitely question many ways of thinking of your own culture. Of course, you will also learn a lot of new things abroad, even in foreign languages. But please take the time already and get familiar with the new language before you leave. We promise you, it's worth it!

Chapter 17 – Bonus – Writing an e-mail

Maybe you need to make an appointment or write an e-mail to the manager of the hotel you are staying in, or maybe you are writing to your friend in Germany. In this chapter, we show you how to properly write an e-mail in German.

A formal letter

Start your letter with the word "Sehr geehrte/r Herr/Frau" followed by the last name of the person you are writing to. For example:

Sehr geehrter Herr Schmidt,

Sehr geehrte Frau Schmidt,

Here are some things you could write:

Danke für … - Thanks for your …

Ihren Brief - letter

Ihre Postkarte - postcard

Ihr Geschenk - present

Ihre Einladung - invitation

Entschuldigen Sie bitte, dass ich mir mit der Antwort so lange Zeit gelassen habe. - Sorry it's taken me so long to write.

Ich hoffe es geht Ihnen gut. - I hope you're well.

Es war schön, Sie letzte Woche zu sehen. - Good to see you again last week.

Ich freue mich Sie bald wieder zu sehen. - Look forward to seeing you soon!

Here are some ways to finish a formal letter:

Alles Gute, - Best regards,

Viele Grüße, - Kind regards,

End the letter with your last name.

Write an E-Mail

E-mails, whether business or private, are usually written in a more informal style than letters.

You should always give your email a subject that describes its purpose in a few words.

There are different guidelines for how business emails should be started. However, it is common to use the first name in both business and private emails, as long as you know the recipient.

It is not necessary to use "Lieber" (Dear), although some prefer this. Generally, business emails should be kept short. If you are sending, remember to mention them in the text of your e-mail. To end a private email, you can use the same expressions as for informal letters. There are different guidelines for how you should end your business emails. In general, the following expressions are appropriate:

Gruß, - Regards,

Freundliche Grüße, - Kind regards,

Mit besten Grüßen, - Best regards,

Mit freundlichen Grüßen, - With kind regards,

In business emails, you should continue to add your full name, organization, and contact information at the end.

Write a formal e-mail

If you know the addressee's name, start your letter with Sehr geehrter Herr (for a man), Sehr geehrte Frau (for a woman), followed by the surname.

Here are some things you could write in a formal e-mail:

Ich beziehe mich in diesem Schreiben auf Ihren Brief vom 4. September, bezüglich Ihrer unbezahlten Rechnung. - I am writing in reply to your letter of 4 September regarding your outstanding invoice.

Bezug nehmend auf unser Gespräch möchte ich gerne unseren Termin am Dienstag, 7. Januar um 09:30 Uhr bestätigen. - Further to our conversation, I'm pleased to confirm our appointment for 9.30am on Tuesday, 7 January.

Ich wäre Ihnen sehr dankbar, wenn Sie sich der Angelegenheit baldmöglichst annehmen würden. - I would be grateful if you could attend to this matter as soon as possible.

Wenn Sie weitere Informationen wünschen, zögern Sie bitte nicht, sich mit mir in Verbindung zu setzen. - If you would like any further information, please don't hesitate to contact me.

If you want an answer, you can use one of the following expressions at the end of your letter:

Ich freue mich darauf, von Ihnen zu hören. - I look forward to hearing from you.

If you started the letter with Sehr geehrter Herr/Frau, you should finish it as follows:

Mit freundlichen Grüßen, - Yours sincerely,

Mit freundlichen Grüßen, - Yours faithfully,

Add your signature at the end, followed by your full name.

Conclusion

Learning a language perfectly in two weeks on vacation is impossible. So it's not worth trying? Maybe you also believe that your language skills are not good enough to speak to the locals. You're wrong!

No matter how well you speak the language, even a short vacation can be a real boost for your language skills. But you have to do it right. Just going on holiday and watching what "happens" will usually lead to disappointment.

So how do you manage to get the most out of your vacation, no matter how low or high your language level is? Before traveling abroad, you should make the right preparations. So you make sure that it really works. The more you speak German on your holiday, the more you'll be comfortable with the language.

Sometimes talking to locals can be extremely difficult, especially if your language level is not quite as high. It can happen that people have no patience with you to have a conversation. Nevertheless, there are many ways to talk to the locals in the local language. It does not always have to be highly complex conversations. There are also opportunities to have short and easy talks, because even those help you with your language skills.

As a beginner or if you are not so sure about the language, you should have a short and simple conversation. This works best with people who have no other choice but to talk to you – like the waiter in restaurants, a barkeeper, receptionists in hotels, couriers and similar.

This is why you'll have everything you need in this book. You have to insist on speaking in the local language. If not, explain briefly that you would like to practice the language a bit. Almost everyone will understand.

And lastly, don't be afraid. It's okay to make mistakes. Everyone makes them. Make sure you don't forget this phrasebook on your trip and you'll be fine!

Made in the USA
Coppell, TX
21 July 2020